IT IS
WELL
WITH
MY SOUL

Other Books by Shelly Beach

Ambushed by Grace:
Help and Hope on the Caregiving Journey

Precious Lord, Take My Hand:
Meditations for Caregivers

MEDITATIONS *for* THOSE LIVING *with*
ILLNESS, PAIN, *and the* CHALLENGES *of* AGING

I T I S
W E L L
WITH
M Y S O U L

S HELLY B EACH

DISCOVERY HOUSE
PUBLISHERS®

It Is Well with My Soul: Meditations for Those Living with Illness, Pain, and the Challenges of Aging

© 2012 by Shelly Beach

Discovery House is affiliated with RBC Ministries, Grand Rapids, Michigan.

Requests for permission to quote from this book should be directed to: Permissions Department, Discovery House Publishers, P.O. Box 3566, Grand Rapids, MI 49501, or contact us by e-mail at permissionsdept@dhp.org

All Scripture quotations, unless otherwise indicated, are taken from the Holy Bible, New International Version®, NIV®. Copyright © 1973, 1978, 1984 by Biblica, Inc.™ Used by permission of Zondervan. All rights reserved worldwide. www.zondervan.com

The persons and events portrayed in this book have been used with permission. To protect the privacy of individuals, some names have been changed.

Interior design by Nick Richardson

Library of Congress Cataloging-in-Publication Data
Beach, Shelly.
It is well with my soul : meditations for those living with illness, pain, and the challenges of aging / Shelly Beach.
    pages   cm

ISBN 978-1-57293-574-7

1. Sick—Prayers and devotions. 2. Suffering—Prayers and devotions. 3. Older people—Prayers and devotions. I. Title.
BV4910.B425   2012   242'.4—dc23   2012028201

Printed in the United States of America

Second printing in 2013

Contents

Section 6: Lies, Legacies, and Letting Go

Appendixes

"It Is Well with My Soul"

By Horatio Spafford

When peace, like a river, attendeth my way,
When sorrows like sea billows roll;
Whatever my lot, Thou has taught me to say,
It is well, it is well with my soul.

Refrain:
It is well with my soul,
It is well, it is well with my soul.

Though Satan should buffet, though trials should come,
Let this blest assurance control,
That Christ has regarded my helpless estate,
And hath shed His own blood for my soul.

My sin—O, the bliss of this glorious thought—
My sin not in part but the whole,
Is nailed to the cross, and I bear it no more,
Praise the Lord, praise the Lord, O my soul!

For me, be it Christ, be it Christ hence to live:
If Jordan above me shall roll,
No pang shall be mine, for in death as in life,
Thou wilt whisper Thy peace to my soul.
But, Lord, 'tis for Thee, for Thy coming we wait,
The sky, not the grave, is our goal;
Oh, trump of the angel! Oh, voice of the Lord!
Blessed hope, blessed rest of my soul!

And, Lord, haste the day when my faith shall be sight,
The clouds be rolled back as a scroll;
The trump shall resound and the Lord shall descend,
"Even so"—it is well with my soul.

INTRODUCTION

My husband Dan pulled me from the front seat of our aging 1990 Impala station wagon, and I crumpled like a rag doll into his arms. His hands were gentle as he slid me into a waiting wheelchair and pushed me through the doors of the emergency room of Detroit Medical Center (DMC). I'd slumped in a heap beside him for the two-hour drive from the small hospital where I'd been released to DMC, where my family had demanded I be transferred. I'd prayed my way through each mile of the trip, with my eyes shut tight against a world spinning out of control as I'd clutched my retching stomach.

I'm not sure I'll ever know why the doctor in the previous hospital seemed ornery and offended that my family asked for me to be transferred to a hospital specializing in brain surgery. It would be easy to assume it was ego or injured pride. Perhaps it was a bad burrito or ingrown toenail. Whatever the reason, he'd refused to order an ambulance, so Dan had been forced to load his hurling wife into our car, steer with one hand, and assist with the plastic basin I was clutching to my chest (my lovely parting gift) for the two-hour trip.

Something deep in my soul that June of 1999 told me that, in spite of what three doctors in three different hospitals had told me, I was critically sick.

It seemed impossible that just days before, I'd been herding a group of energetic high school students through Europe on a tour of London, Paris, and Rome. Then one second of skull-shattering, searing pain had changed everything about my life. My forty-four-year-old body had crumpled to the ground, and my life had divided into *before* and *after.*

I'd returned to my London hotel room and stumbled to the bed with a throbbing headache, and when I stood to my feet an hour later, the left side of my face was drooping and my gait was unsteady. By morning I was feeling better, and I led my students on a five-mile walking tour of the city.

But twenty-four hours later, after flying back home to the States, before I'd had time to put away my passport or unpack my toothbrush, waves of nausea had slammed into my body with tsunami force. Within hours, my unsteady legs buckled beneath me. Simply opening my eyes sent me retching. Even my eyes betrayed me as my vision went double.

Everything about life had changed, and I'd become as useless as a piece of lint—unable to see, stand, walk, or even move to scratch an itch.

Brain Gone AWOL

Dan insisted I see a doctor. Since it was a weekend and our family doc was unavailable, he whisked me off to our hometown emergency room. After a ten-minute evaluation, the doctor sent me home with a smile and a diagnosis of an inner ear infection and Bell's palsy—a dysfunctional facial nerve—that he believed explained the droop that had overtaken the left side of my face.

But as the day wore on, my nausea intensified, and I was soon vomiting faster than a minnow can swim a dipper. (If you have never seen a minnow swim a dipper, just know you should be very impressed.) So the following morning, Dan took me to ER Number Two at a slightly larger hospital. This doctor echoed the diagnosis of the previous doctor and sent me home with a smile, another bill, antibiotics, and a promise that I'd feel better in a few days.

In spite of promises and antibiotics, I was feeling sicker by the hour, and guiltier because I was now throwing up pricey drugs and piling up hospital bills faster than those dipper-swimming minnows. Hour by hour, my body grew more out of control. Not long after we arrived home from ER Number Two, my eyeballs began to tremble. Truly alarmed, Dan called our family physician at home. She met us at her office but barely glanced at me before ordering me to ER Number Three in a larger city an hour east of us.

As sick as I was, I felt a strange sense of relief as we headed for the hospital. I was sure the doctors there would give us answers. And although my intensifying symptoms terrified me, I hoped they'd lead the doctors to the right diagnosis.

At ER Number Three, the doctor's demeanor reflected concern. He immediately ordered a CT scan and an MRI that imaged my brain in detail. By this time, family members had gathered to support us. As we all waited for test results, I tried not to think about the possible diagnoses.

Stroke.

Aneurysm.

And, of course, the Big C, brain cancer.

Just weeks before, a cousin my age had been admitted to the same hospital with a brain tumor, and although it was found to be benign, she'd required surgery that had left her with permanent limitations. Another cousin two years older than I had recently suffered a severe stroke. My mother had also had strokes, and my father had suffered a number of transient ischemic attacks, or mini-strokes. I found myself suddenly wishing I could switch out my medical chart for someone else's.

I knew one thing for sure: my neurological condition was deteriorating. I lay in a fetal position in my hospital bed, praying that perhaps I'd had only a small stroke and could soon go home and focus on getting well again.

But when the doctor came into my room holding my file, the look on his blurred face (both of them) told me the news was ominous. I struggled to understand his words through the fog that had overtaken my brain.

Tests showed a bleed in the center of my brain, as well as a large lesion near my brain stem in a location the doctor described as "troublesome." Without further tests, it was impossible to know whether or not the lesion was a tumor, inflammation, or something else. The only way to find answers, he stated, was to crack open my skull to investigate.

Crack open my skull? And noodle around in my brain?

I could barely absorb the words. Dan and my family members were in shock. Just the day before, a doctor had shooed me out of the emergency room to make room for really sick people. Now I was being told a doctor wanted to go gallivanting through my gray matter.

Even with clouded thinking I found his suggestion to drill through my skull and cavort through my cranium at a mid-sized hospital with a mid-sized reputation for medical success . . . disquieting. But before my brain could muster the strength to express my alarm, my family spoke up on my behalf and asked that I be transferred to Detroit Medical Center—the only hospital in Michigan performing Gamma Knife brain surgery in 1999. Just in case.

I didn't know what a gamma knife was, and as Dan made plans for my transfer, I prayed I'd never find out.

Life in Hospital Land

Soon after Dan rolled me through the doors of Detroit Medical Center, life shifted into another strange, new reality. I measured time in increments between blood draws, doctors' visits, and occasional swigs of food supplements. My former life as a wife and teacher became a dim memory. My connection to friends and loved ones (most of whom lived hours away and could seldom visit) faded, as I sank into foggy awareness in Room 312. The familiar world I'd known melted away and was replaced by pain, dependency, isolation, and uncertainty. With one mind-jarring jolt, I'd changed from a confident wife, mother, teacher, author, and travel guide to a patient unable to read a book, tie her shoes, bathe herself, or lift a fork to her own mouth.

What was even more frightening was that no one could tell me what was wrong with me or how much my body and mind would degenerate. I was struggling to think, swallow, and breathe. For the first time in my life, I felt completely helpless, knowing I could do nothing to influence my future.

Little did I know how painful the days ahead would become. And little did I know how I would treasure them for changing my life.

Face-to-Face with the Father

For the first forty-four years of my life, I'd used a tried-and-true approach to chaos, pain, or tragedy: run and hide, or manipulate the people or circumstances around me. When I became ill, that approach failed completely. God pulled me away from my distractions and placed me in a situation I couldn't flee or fix so I could look into His face and discover who He really was.

Over the past dozen years or so, God has used illness to teach me dependency on Him and sweet, soul-stretching lessons of interdependency on others. I'm grateful for the prayers of friends who have prayed for my total healing. I've prayed for it, too. But sickness has taught me I'm not in control. My brain lesion reminds me God's hand is resting daily upon my shoulder, and He is near. Illness has taught me the principle of diminishment taught in John 3:30: "He must increase, but I must decrease" (KJV).

Perhaps, like me, you've experienced fear or loss of control with a devastating diagnosis in your life. You may be facing the challenges of aging or life transitions. Perhaps you feel helpless, hopeless, or as though you don't have the strength to face what lies ahead. Whatever difficulties you may be facing, I want you to know you're not alone.

This book was written to help you with the challenges of chronic pain, illness, life transitions, loss, or end-of-life issues. Whatever sorrow, trial, burden, or heartache may be yours, this book was written to give you hope and comfort, to let you share in the experiences of others who have walked a similar path, and to draw you close to your heavenly Father, who cares about your every tear and heartache.

The book presents meditations on a wide range of topics: anger, grief, depression, joy, grace, the role of advocates, and many other subjects. The devotional material is enriched with prayers, journaling questions, and a collection of practical appendices. Read through his book prayerfully, spending time alone with God, asking that He reveal His heart to you.

My prayer for you today is that, above all, you will find new intimacy with God in your faith journey and come to know and trust the one who sent His Son to redeem our pain, give purpose to even our darkest moments, and offer His intimate and personal love to us.

Devastation, Doubt, and Deliverance

When peace, like a river, attendeth my way,
When sorrows like sea billows roll;
Whatever my lot, Thou has taught me to say,
It is well, it is well, with my soul.

It is well with my soul,
It is well, it is well with my soul.

You cannot make yourself feel something you do not feel, but you can make yourself do right in spite of your feelings.

PEARL BUCK

If any of my friends tried to call me a few weeks back, they probably didn't have much luck getting through. I wasn't in a chatty mood.

My newly engaged and only daughter Jessica was missing her mother, and I was heartsick because I couldn't hop a plane to Seattle to spoil her as she tore through legal pads making wedding plans.

The same week Jess called, our lawn mower went belly-up, our well pump gave up the ghost, and our septic tank announced it was full by transforming our toilets into disturbingly memorable fountains.

And if that wasn't enough, a much-anticipated book deal I'd thrown myself into went down in flames. If we owned a cat, I'd have kicked it. (Um . . . not *really*. We writers call this *hyperbole*. Animal rights activists need not fear.) I let my attitude slide into the Dumpster and gave my husband fair warning to take cover. I *felt* lousy, so I told myself my life *was* lousy, and I was entitled to a pity party, complete with truckloads of carbs, ownership of the TV remote, and a victim attitude.

Letting Emotions Run the Show

Today's consumer-driven culture tells us we deserve to get what we want *now*. And when we get tired of what we have, we're entitled to "trade up" to something (or someone) newer and better. Even pastors and faith leaders often echo this me-first philosophy. For instance, on a September 2011 TV broadcast, televangelist Pat Robertson stated that people married to spouses with Alzheimer's should consider them "dead," divorce them, and start new lives (http://abcn.ws/qlioXd).

However, the Bible teaches a different paradigm—not just regarding marriage, but for all of life. Jesus modeled this worldview for His followers: "Greater love has no one than this: to lay down one's life . . ." (John 15:13 TNIV). When every shred of human emotion and logic cried out for Jesus to walk away from suffering, loved compelled Him to lay down His life for those He loved.

Nearly a century and a half ago, a man named Horatio Spafford experienced excruciating loss. When every shred of human emotion and logic cried out for Spafford to deny his faith and his God, he, instead, fled into the arms of the God he loved. In his hour of deepest pain, Spafford poured out an expression of worship and penned the beloved hymn "It Is Well with My Soul."

But where did Spafford find faith to trust God when, like Job, loss upon loss pummeled his soul?

Undaunted in Devastation

A successful lawyer, businessman, and friend of evangelist D. L. Moody, Horatio Spafford lived a life of both affluence and influence. He, his wife Anna, a son, and four daughters lived in comfort in Chicago in the 1860s where he invested heavily in real estate along the Lake Michigan shoreline.

But in 1870, Spafford's fortunes suddenly reversed. Tragically, his four-year-old son contracted scarlet fever and died. The following year, the Great Chicago Fire wiped out the family real estate holdings, and the Spaffords lost everything. For two years, he and his wife worked tirelessly to help rebuild the city of Chicago, but in 1873, Spafford decided the family needed a rest and change of scenery. His plan was to take a European vacation and assist D. L. Moody and musician Ira Sankey with a London evangelistic outreach.

The family traveled to New York City, where they were scheduled to set sail for England on the *Ville de Havre*. Before their departure, Spafford received word that he was needed back in Chicago to finalize a business deal. He sent Anna and his four daughters ahead aboard the *Ville de Havre* while he returned home, promising to join them as quickly as possible.

Never could Horatio Spafford have foreseen the consequences of his last-minute decision. Nine days after arriving in Chicago, he received a cable from his wife: "Saved alone." A passing ship struck the *Ville de Havre*, sinking it in just twelve minutes and claiming the lives of 226 people. Anna had struggled helplessly as all four of their daughters were torn from her arms by the waves and drowned— Annie, Maggie, Bessie, and Tanetta. A floating plank caught beneath Anna's unconscious body and kept her afloat just long enough for rescue efforts to reach her.

Horatio Spafford raced to New York City and boarded the next ship for the sea crossing to join his wife. As a courtesy, the ship's captain called him to the bridge to inform him they were passing over the spot where Spafford's daughters had drowned. He stood silently with the captain for a short time, and then returned to his cabin, where he sat in solitude and penned the words to the beloved hymn "It Is Well with My Soul."

Horatio Spafford chose a text that shows a mother's response to her son's death. In 2 Kings 4:18–20, a Shunammite woman's only child has just died in her lap. Her mother's heart is crushed. The loss is devastating, and Scripture states that her "soul is vexed within her" (v. 27 KJV). In spite of her pain and wrenching grief, she chooses to express that, although her soul is mourning deeply, "it is well" (v. 26 KJV). Horatio Spafford drew inspiration, and most likely comfort, from this woman's response.

A Deeper Look

Like Horatio Spafford, some of you may have experienced the gut-wrenching grief of losing a child. Or perhaps you've lost a spouse or dear friend or are facing a life-challenging diagnosis. One certainty in life is that we all face sorrows associated with death, illness, aging, and diminishment. And in the struggle and pain of life, we often battle with bitterness, doubt, anger, and wonder "Why me?"

Horatio Spafford lost his only son. He lost his financial security. In one sweeping blow, he lost his remaining children. Yet in the freshest moments of his grief, as he passed over the very site of his daughters' tragic deaths, he penned an anthem of peace and confidence—a public statement of his faith in a trustworthy God. Each stroke of his pen etched part of a faith anthem that told the world his story:

When sorrow comes, God is enough.

When life throws its worst at me, God is enough.

When Satan attacks, God is enough.

When sin overwhelms me, God is enough.

When I feel like a failure, God is enough.

Spafford could have chosen the easy way out. He could have turned his back on his God, abandoned his wife, played the "Why me?" card, justified bitterness, retreated into himself, and claimed all of it was God's fault. Instead, he chose to express his pain with an affirmation of faith in a faithful God.

Spafford used the pain of his life to draw closer to God and to move forward. His hymn "It Is Well with My Soul" teaches us valuable lessons about how to approach suffering. Let's examine three ways.

Horatio Spafford acknowledged the reality of his pain. Spafford didn't hide or minimize the fact that he was deeply hurting. In fact, his hymn opens with an expression of his grief. He not only admitted his pain, he expressed his sorrow in a powerful word picture of the relentless pounding of crushing waves: "when sorrows like sea billows roll." He linked his grief to the grief of those who would hear his hymn and called them to acknowledge the persistent, powerful nature of sorrow, like the surf endlessly slamming against the shore.

I was once on a ship in a storm at sea, surrounded by thirty-foot swells. Miles from shore, we were slammed again and again by powerful waves that sent us into the depths of troughs. The sheer size and endless pounding of the waves nearly drove me to panic.

Do you suffer with chronic pain? Do you know the disappointment of diminished ability? Has illness so complicated life that a spouse has abandoned you? The pain of our lives often makes us feel as though we're alone at sea, surrounded by raging mountains of water that could submerge us at any moment. With the brushstrokes of just a few words, Spafford described his grief in the loss of his family: "sorrows like sea billows." Yet, like a master artist, he illuminates the picture with the light of hope in a faithful God.

Horatio Spafford used his negative experience to tell others about God's power to provide peace in the storms of life. The saying goes that we have only one opportunity to make a first impression. The first things we choose to say and do often communicate who we are and what we believe. In the midst of his grief and loss, Horatio Spafford chose to make the first words he penned positive—to remind people that God's peace is constant and certain, no matter the circumstances that surge around us. With his opening words, "When peace like a river attendeth my way," he stated his view of life: this world will pound us with heartache, but we have hope and peace in God.

Horatio Spafford experienced peace in the present moments of the storm because he'd learned to trust God in the past. Spafford had built a relationship of trust with God over time. "Whatever my lot, Thou *has taught* me to say . . ." Spafford and his wife had already lost a son. He'd survived both the Chicago business world and the Great Chicago Fire. He'd learned from his life experiences—both positive and painful—to rely on God. "I have learned to be content whatever the circumstances" (Philippians 4:11). Interestingly, the Greek word translated "content" carries the meaning of "self-sufficiency," or one who is not in need. In other words, although Spafford's circumstances might have looked like losses to those around him, he needed nothing because he found his sufficiency in God.

The Secrets of Attending

We all will face storms that will threaten our faith: an unexpected diagnosis, the loss of a loved one, alienation and loneliness, anxiety regarding the future, financial crisis, loss of dreams or hope for the future. Perhaps you live with chronic pain or illness, or chafe because you're growing more dependent upon others to do the things you were once able to do yourself. You may be frustrated or even angry about freedoms you've been forced to relinquish and the choices you must make as you transition into a different stage of life. Perhaps it's difficult for you to say, "It is well with my soul."

If you're struggling, you're not alone. In fact, few people know that in the latter part of his life—after suffering loss upon loss and pressing on to serve God on the mission field—Horatio Spafford struggled, too. David, a man after God's own heart; Solomon, the wisest man in the world; the apostle Paul, a New Testament church leader; and other "heroes of the faith" show us that struggle is part of the life of faith for all of us.

My prayer is that you will learn from others who walked through storms and learned to say, "It is well with my soul." May you draw strength and joy in learning about God's passionate heart of love for you.

Sovereignty and Suffering

We are afflicted in every way, but not crushed; perplexed,
but not driven to despair; persecuted, but not forsaken; struck down,
but not destroyed; always carrying in the body the death of Jesus, so that the
life of Jesus may also be manifested in our bodies. For we who live are always
being given over to death for Jesus' sake, so that the life of Jesus also may be
manifested in our mortal flesh.

2 Corinthians 4:8–11 (ESV)

C. S. Lewis has said, "God whispers to us in our pleasures, speaks to us in our conscience, but shouts in our pains: It is His megaphone to rouse a deaf world" (*The Problem of Pain*, 1940). Physical suffering speaks loudly in a world addicted to comfort and pleasure, and God uses it to speak, not only to us personally, but to the world around us. Our suffering is never personal. It is always God speaking to anyone willing to listen.

Within weeks of her eighth birthday, my god-daughter Alicia underwent her fortieth brain surgery for complications from cerebral palsy. She's lived most of her life in a pediatric neurological center hours from her home, with her mother at her side but separated from her father and three siblings. Life for Alicia's family and other families like hers who live with chronic or critical illness are challenging in ways most of us struggle to understand: isolation from friends, separation from family, continual pain, invasive medical procedures, unpredictable body changes, an erratic social life, a frequently interrupted education, and the restrictions of a disease, as well as other complicating factors.

Another friend's life was changed forever by an accident. As a teenager, Jill was a competitive gymnast with an eye on the Olympics. During a gymnastic practice, she was instructed to attempt a back flip on a trampoline, but she fell short of a full rotation and landed on her neck, breaking it in two places. At the age of fourteen, Jill was confined to life in a wheelchair as a quadriplegic.

God also used my friend Johnny and his family to speak to the world. Early in the spring of 2010, seven-year-old Johnny was diagnosed with an inoperable and rare brain cancer called pontine glioma (DIPG). On Monday he was competing in field day at school in Arkansas. On Friday he was a patient at St. Jude Children's Research Hospital in Memphis, Tennessee. "Johnny the Brave" fought valiantly for just under a year before he lost the battle with cancer.

Some questions in life seem too tough for answers. Why does God allow children to suffer and die? Why doesn't He always cure the people we love? Why do natural disasters, famines, and disease wipe out millions in our world? Because we're image-bearers of a just and loving heavenly Father, our hearts cry out for resolution to the pain of our broken world. We long for answers we can understand, but the truth is, because we're humans, we can only know and comprehend within the limits of human understanding. We're not God. Our world is broken beyond our understanding.

When Adam and Eve, our first parents, sinned, they released the consequences of evil into the world, and every generation—man, woman, and child—has lived with the consequences. Our only hope is to trust a God greater than evil, greater than our sin, and greater than our limited intellect, who promises to use all things for our good—even our suffering. And although life often seems far from just or fair, God promises His sovereign plan is at work, in spite of what we see from our limited perspective. In fact, He loved us so much, He ordained suffering for His own Son, whom He loved beyond anything we can think or imagine, to redeem our suffering.

Are you struggling through pain and questioning God's sovereignty? Don't despair. God is with you, as He was with His own Son Jesus in His suffering, working out a plan that will redeem even our deepest pain.

Dearest Father, You hate to see Your children suffer, but You have promised to use everything to bring glory to yourself and work out Your eternal plan in the world. Help me to trust You even in those moments when I cannot feel You, Father. When the pain threatens to overwhelm me, help me rest in Your unfailing love and mercy. May your praise continually be on my lips. My only hope is in You. Amen.

1. When has God used pain to speak to you in your circumstances? What did you learn?

2. In what ways have you seen God use suffering to bring hope to the world or to glorify himself?

LAMENT

Yea, though I walk through the valley of the shadow of death, I will fear no evil: for thou art with me; thy rod and thy staff they comfort me.

PSALM 23:4 (KJV)

Most of us waltz through life under the illusion that we have the power to shape our futures and control our destinies. Nothing destroys the illusion that we are autonomous and independent creatures more quickly than illness.

My life looked a lot like the American dream in 1999. I was married to the love of my life, had two healthy kids, and was lucky enough to travel the world leading high school students on travel-study tours. In early June, I was concluding a trip to London, Paris, and Rome when a bizarre headache struck. Seventy-two hours later, back in the States, I lay tucked in a fetal position in the neuro-oncology unit of Detroit Medical Center.

Soon I became the subject of a hospital-wide game of "Stump the Doctors," as physicians across several departments attempted to diagnose the walnut-sized lesion they'd found near my brain stem. Each day, after a new round of tests, my doctor reeled off new lists of illnesses I *didn't* have, including cancer or a tumor. But doctors could only guess what my lesion actually *was*—perhaps a virus or infection. With each day that passed, the symptoms grew worse.

Although my family refused to leave my side, I felt isolated and alone. No one could walk this path with me, and in the darkness and silence, I wrestled with fear and anger.

Would I ever leave the hospital? Walk again? Bathe myself? Enjoy a meal with my family? Would I see my son and daughter settled in life or meet their spouses, if they married? Would I teach again, travel, read, or do anything more than lie motionless and struggle against an eroding body?

I fought against anger for the relentless pain gripping my body, for being cut off from the life I'd always known and the future I'd always envisioned as fear, grief, sorrow, and disappointment washed over me. In my pain, I struggled with guilt for not being "spiritual enough" to face my circumstances with unquestioning faith and resiliency.

Years later I began to understand the importance of lament, of expressing our hurt and disappointment to God. The "lament" psalms show us God listens to our cries and cares about our sorrows. He longs for us to come to Him with our broken hearts and disappointments. For instance, David, the writer of Psalm 12, tells God how people have disappointed him: "Help, Lord, for no one is faithful anymore; those who are loyal have vanished from the human race" (v. 1 TNIV). He writes about the frustrations of his enemies in Psalm 6: "All night long I flood my bed with weeping and drench my couch with tears. My eyes grow weak with sorrow; they fail because of all my foes" (vv. 6–7).

When we experience pain, we're often tempted to accuse or doubt God. We can feel like God doesn't care or can't be in control and can respond by accusing Him of not caring and causing our pain. We justify our grumbling and complaining, wallow in self-serving attitudes, indulge in self-pity, and get angry. Recently I met a man at a book signing event who'd walked away from his faith because his wife had divorced him. From his perspective, his divorce was all God's fault.

Scriptural lament teaches something quite different. Lament psalms encourage us to freely express our sorrow and pain to God. We're never asked to deny the hurt we're experiencing but, instead, to take our hurts *to* God as our source of strength. Lament offers us the freedom to express our pain and to appeal for relief. It is the only safe place to confess our sins and to be comforted, knowing our pleas are heard by a God of mercy, not a God who abandons us in our suffering.

The writer of Psalm 43 asks God to plead his cause, to show up and rescue him in his unjust circumstances. The psalmist even asks God why He's rejected him. But while the writer freely expresses his pain, he returns to the unchanging character of God: "Put your hope in God, for I will yet praise him, my Savior and my God" (v. 5).

What heartache are you experiencing today? Bring that heartache to God and ask for mercy. Your loving Father stands waiting with open arms, ready to listen.

Father, I am hurting, and my pain is beyond my comprehension. I ask for healing of my body, soul, and mind, and for protection from bitterness and anger in this deep place of pain in my life. I turn to You as my source of protection and provision. In this moment of grief and loss, I choose to praise You as the loving God who even now is cradling me in His arms. Amen.

1. Have you ever felt fearful of expressing your anger or hurt to God because you thought it might be unspiritual? How can you

express your pain to God and appeal to Him for relief without accusing Him?

2. When have you felt a desire to pour out a lament to God? In what circumstances? How has lament helped you strengthen your faith?

DIAGNOSIS

So do not fear, for I am with you; do not be dismayed, for I am your God.
I will strengthen you and help you; I will uphold you with my
righteous right hand.

ISAIAH 41:10

Nights in the neuro-oncology unit terrified me most. From dawn until midnight, my husband, Dan, kept my fears at bay as he kept vigil at my side. The warmth of his hand encasing mine helped me screen out the pain and vomiting, and the cycle of procedures and tests that marked each new day of my stay. I hated the evening hours—the countdown to midnight and the moment my weary husband kissed me good night and headed off to catch a few hours' sleep before returning for another day of waiting and praying.

Each night after Dan left, I steeled my mind against the terrifying realities pressing against my soul. I'd been admitted to my third hospital in less than a week. I'd been evaluated by half a dozen doctors who'd administered dozens of tests, yet no one could tell me what was wrong with me.

We did know several things for sure. We knew a person could vomit every twenty minutes and still live. The nurses had given me the nickname "The Puking Lady in Room 316." We knew something big and nasty had appeared near my brain stem and was causing a ruckus. And we knew a strange little blood vessel (called a vascular malformation) had decided to wimp out and leak in my brain.

I'd been tucked into tubes, prodded and poked, even duct-taped to one machine when my limp and lifeless muscles couldn't support me to stand. Just thinking exhausted me. With each new day, I felt myself slipping further away. By my second week at Detroit Medical Center, I could tolerate only occasional sips of a dietary supplement, and my body ached from being locked into a fetal position.

Still doctors were baffled as they debated my diagnosis. I was sent to see a specialist in multiple sclerosis. Doctors searched for a primary site for metastatic cancer. I was tested for Guillain-Barré syndrome. Each day the results came back negative.

Not knowing what was wrong with me terrified me, and nights were the worst. My neuro-oncologist was a dedicated man who often made his rounds past midnight, just minutes after Dan left for the night. Each night I braced myself to hear the dreaded diagnosis: brain cancer. But in God's providence, a diagnosis never came. More than ten years later, after treatment that greatly improved my condition, doctors still remain puzzled. Today I live with chronic symptoms that mimic multiple sclerosis, as well as other neurological oddities.

A diagnosis can cut us off from the expectation of fulfilled hopes and dreams and sentence us to an uncertain or dreaded future. But diagnosis and illness do not cut us off from the presence of God and our assurance of His control in all things. God's love and oversight in my life are not limited by illness or circumstances. In fact, He *uses* circumstances to work out things for my good—purposes and plans that surpass my human understanding. My illness became a means to spiritual growth that led to opportunities to speak into the lives of thousands of people across the nation. My illness has given me opportunities to collaborate with songwriters, filmmakers, and other authors, and to speak in the nation's prisons. However, it's not necessary for us to see the visible evidence of God's work; He invests our every single tear to work out His will on our behalf.

If you're a child of God, hope for your future isn't based on what you see or don't see, but on the unchanging character of God, your loving Father, who knows and sees all and holds you securely in the palm of His hand.

Dear God, sometimes I dread my doctors' appointments, not knowing what lies ahead. But You charted my course and numbered my days long before I was even conceived. A doctor's words do not limit Your love or Your plan for me. Help me to trust You, in spite of the challenges that lie ahead. Help me to praise You, not necessarily for all things, but in all things. Amen.

1. Has God used a medical diagnosis to change your life? To draw you closer to Him? In what ways?

2. Have you doubted God's sovereignty in the tough times? How have you dealt with the difficult questions and doubts?

DOUBT

Give thanks to the Lord, for he is good, and his loyal love endures!
Let those delivered by the Lord speak out, those whom he delivered from the
power of the enemy, and gathered from foreign lands, from east and west,
from north and south. They wandered through the wilderness on a desert road;
they found no city in which to live. They were hungry and thirsty;
they fainted from exhaustion. They cried out to the Lord in their distress;
he delivered them from their troubles.

PSALM 107:1–6 (NET)

I f we're honest, we'll admit that at times it can be hard to believe in God's goodness, especially when we or someone we love lives with chronic pain or illness. Many of us have prayed for release from constant pain or for healing, and we wonder how a good God could allow His children to endure what seems to be unbearable and unrelenting suffering.

But many of us also hurt in nonphysical ways. For instance, we may not be blessed with supportive families or churches. Complications from our illness may have driven spouses or children from our lives, and we may receive minimal or no help from family and friends. Chronic sickness often brings financial pressures, and we may be forced to choose between filling prescriptions and paying household utility bills.

In tough times, we ask tough questions. Trials often bring doubts about God and our faith. Doubting God can be a two-edged sword. It can be a catalyst to our faith, stirring us to explore what we believe and come to even deeper levels of understanding, conviction, reflection, and introspection. But doubts can also seduce us into anger and bitterness and lead us to abandon hope and faith.

So is doubt a bad thing? Should we push away our questions?

God is never surprised or insulted by our questions. David questioned God. Job questioned God. And even Jesus questioned God in the garden of Gethsemane before His crucifixion. But at the end of their questioning, David, Job, and Jesus bowed to God's ultimate goodness and sovereignty. They rested in His character as the only answer to the paradox of pain.

Mary, the mother of Jesus, also wrestled with doubt. And why wouldn't she? God's plan for her future seemed ludicrous. Pregnancy without marriage would mean humiliation, alienation, and suffering. God gave her the opportunity to wrestle with her doubts regarding His plan for her future. In seconds, she responded and bowed to the sovereignty of the God she trusted. She said, "I am the Lord's servant. May it be to me as you have said" (Luke 1:38).

Our questions and doubts about God's sovereignty ultimately result in one of four responses: 1) rejecting God as good; 2) rejecting God for other gods; 3) rejecting God for the god of myself; 4) bowing to God's sovereignty.

Are you doubting God for your future? Struggling to trust Him for today? Afraid to trust Him with someone you love or a circumstance beyond your control? Know that you stand with David, Job, and Jesus himself in your struggle.

But may your desire be to respond as they all did—in submission and faith—and to trust in the sovereign God who loves you. May you, too, find the strength and peace like Mary to say, "I am the Lord's servant. May it be to me as you have said."

Dear Father, You know that at times I struggle with doubt. I see suffering and pain, and I don't understand why You don't put a stop to the ugliness in the world. I struggle against anger sometimes. Help me to submit to Your will, knowing that Your goodness brings justice and purpose to all things that seem irreconcilable in my eyes. Help me to understand that You alone are the measure of truth and justice. Amen.

1. When have you doubted the goodness of God? Why?

2. Have your doubts affected your faith in God? If so, in what ways?

DEVASTATION

May the God of hope fill you with all joy and peace as you trust in him,
so that you may overflow with hope by the power of the Holy Spirit.

ROMANS 15:13

Jill was born with both a love and a talent for gymnastics that drove her to train for the Olympics in every spare minute. By the time she was fourteen, she realized it was unlikely she would achieve her goal, but she still trained regularly. Her mother and father, strong Christians, were in a constant tug-of-war with Jill to keep her priorities in order, making sure she included church and youth group activities in her routine. So during the summer of 1994, they enrolled her in a Christian sports camp in the Ozarks of Missouri.

Instead of being excited, Jill was livid because time at camp would disrupt her strict gymnastic schedule. But Kanakuk Kamp changed Jill's spiritual priorities and renewed her love for God. She came home and began her sophomore year in high school with a new desire to glorify Him. She even began to pray about giving up her beloved gymnastics.

During practice the first week of her sophomore year, Jill was practicing double backflips on the trampoline. Although she didn't feel confident, she practiced the move as her coach instructed.

In one split-second, Jill's life changed forever. She landed on her neck, breaking two vertebrae and paralyzing her from the neck down.

Jill remembers little of the first few weeks following her injury. Her parents delayed telling her the injury was permanent. She's thankful for their decision, believing it helped her focus on her surgery and rehabilitation goals. It wasn't until she arrived at a rehab hospital in Florida that she realized that some patients in the facility had been in treatment for years. The truth began to dawn, and Jill set a goal for herself: she'd walk on Easter, the seven-month anniversary of her injury.

When that day arrived, friends and family waited expectantly with her for the miracle. She went to church, expecting to be healed, but the healing didn't come. She sat up until midnight at home waiting for the miracle. With the dawning of the next day, she realized God had a different plan for her life.

The week after Easter was difficult, and Jill sank into a depression. But as time passed, God reminded her of Scripture: "'For I know the plans I have for you,' declares the Lord, 'plans to prosper you and not to harm you, plans to give you hope and a future'" (Jeremiah 29:11). In the past, Jill had used these verses to assure herself God owed her material and physical prosperity. Now He was using them to reassure her He'd care for her spiritual needs and provide for her in ways that would surpass anything she could imagine.

Jill would be the first person to admit that life in a wheelchair has its challenges. While she sometimes feels overwhelmed as a mother of two young sons, she takes things one day at a time. Her advice? Present your frustrations and trials to the Lord and ask for comfort.

Trust the Lord on a daily basis and watch Him work out His best for your life each day.

> *Dear Father, sometimes my circumstances seem devastating, and I can't see how I can make it through another day. As I share the burdens of my heart, give me a willing spirit to lay down my expectations for what I believe I deserve and to cultivate a heart of gratitude for all You've done for me. Amen.*

1. How do you handle your overwhelming disappointments? How do you feel about Jill's advice to present your frustrations and trials to the Lord and to ask for comfort?

2. What are the special challenges of your circumstances today? Make a list of your frustrations and share them with the Lord.

THE BROKENHEARTED

He heals the brokenhearted and binds up their wounds.

PSALM 147:3

The last thing Lisa was expecting when she answered her phone one April day was for God to show up with a message of hope. After forty-nine years of desperation, she'd given up on hope and on life, and she'd created a suicide plan to back it up.

Lisa couldn't remember a moment in life when she hadn't felt despair. Born into a life of abuse and dysfunction, she'd been forced to take care of others from the time she was a child—her younger brothers and sisters, her mother, other children in the foster care system where she'd been placed when her parents were sent to prison. Her heart was crushed one more time the day a foster father drove her to an abortion clinic after repeated sexual abuse and left her to fend for herself. Over the years she'd learned to ignore her spiritual, emotional, and physical needs. By the age of fourteen, she was living alone on the streets.

Even though things were tough, God placed people in Lisa's life to help provide for her, love her, and tell her about His love. When she was five, a loving grandfather introduced her to Jesus, and in spite of the desperation of her life, she clung to the truth that Jesus loved her.

In her adult years, Lisa created a successful career while she continued to struggle inside. Her parents had come to know Jesus Christ in prison. After their release, Lisa rebuilt relationships with them and even assisted with their care. But the physical and emotional damage of her trauma went unaddressed, and she struggled with depression, nightmares, and self-abusive behaviors.

Then one April afternoon, a business associate called Lisa—a woman who recognized the symptoms of trauma immediately. By the end of their first phone call, Lisa had broken her own rules and poured out the secrets of her life story. Although they lived on opposite sides of the country, weeks later they met when Lisa's associate, now a friend, flew out to meet her. Within months, God provided the funds for Lisa's treatment at a trauma treatment center. Ten days of intensive therapy changed her life forever.

For the first time in her life, Lisa focused on her spiritual, emotional, and physical needs. Her trauma treatment confronted lies with truth and freed her from lies that had enslaved Lisa for nearly fifty years.

God heard the deepest cries of Lisa's soul and sent hope, help, and healing. Today, she carries God's message of healing and hope to women in prison.

God's Word promises us that He hears the cries of the broken-hearted and binds up our wounds. But He requires us to move forward in steps of faith. If Lisa hadn't reached out her hand and trusted God when He sent help, she might still be struggling in despair. Sometimes God shines His hope on our path one ray at a time, lighting the way for small steps of faith that move us out of our past and into His future.

Thank You, Father, for the gifts of healing You pour into our lives. Thank You for lifting us up in our moments of despair. May I be willing to submit my will to Yours in moments of pain. May I recognize that despair is Satan's tool of defeat—a lie intended to prevent me from resting in the truth: You love me, and You have provided every good thing for my need. Hear the cries of my heart in this moment, dear Father. Amen.

1. When has your heart been broken? What hope are you seeking today?

2. What truth has Satan sought to steal from your life? What truth do you believe God wants you to recall today?

NEVER FORSAKEN

Be strong and courageous. Do not be afraid or terrified because of them, for the Lord your God goes with you; he will never leave you nor forsake you.

DEUTERONOMY 31:6

D an and I intended for our visit to be brief—a fifteen minute chat with a friend who'd been diagnosed with a rare and deadly condition. Dave had been admitted to a medical facility in our city that specialized in experimental treatments for his illness. For months, he'd teetered on the brink of death, his condition improving, and then plummeting as the disease flared and attacked his major organs and heart. Over the past year, he'd been forced to step away from his ministry as a pastor.

A man whose twenty-something sons had never defeated him in basketball had been reduced to a bed-bound shut-in. In all the years I'd known Dave, I'd never seen him fear anything. Illness was new territory for him, and, frankly, I wondered if he was afraid.

Dave's condition was so volatile he was rarely able to see visitors, except for his wife and adult children, who provided round-the-clock support. He was staunchly independent and appreciated privacy, so Dan and I expected to chat just few minutes and then leave.

We were surprised to find Dave alone when we arrived. His wife had gone to the cafeteria for a dinner break, and his children had left for the evening. He gave us a summary of his condition, and I commented that my brother shared the same diagnosis and was familiar with the treatment plan.

Dave's eyes widened. He'd never met anyone who'd heard of his illness. Over the next thirty minutes, he poured out details of his emotional battle against death. Each week had brought a new loss. Every drug had brought a negative side-effect. He'd lost bodily functions, and doctors couldn't predict what he might lose next.

Dan and I assured him we knew the dark place of illness and physical loss, and the three of us prayed together with a new intimacy.

As Dan and I were about to leave, a nurse came into the room to administer a newly prescribed drug, and Dave asked if we could stay while it was given. His face tensed as the nurse injected the medication into his IV, and within moments, we knew something was wrong. He gasped for air and tried to speak, but no sound came. The nurse called for the stroke team.

Dave clung to my hand while the medical team worked. Minutes later nurses ushered his wife to his side. Dan and I waited until his condition stabilized before leaving. Two years later, he still speaks of the terror of that moment as his body was swept out of control.

We've all experienced terrorizing moments, and we shouldn't feel shame in fearing the unknown, the painful, or the threatening. Even positive changes like a new job or a move can prompt fears. Unfortunately, Christians can be reluctant to talk about fears because we believe it's "unspiritual" to be afraid.

Fear is a legitimate response when our health and safety are threatened or when the unknown looms before us. What matters most is how we handle our fears—where we take them, and whether we allow them to control us. When we take our fears to God, they can become a catalyst to our spiritual growth and a blessing in the lives of others. Dave believes one of God's purposes for his emotional roller-coaster ride of ill health was to enrich his ministry. A year later, he returned to the pulpit, his ministry transformed by his experience. He wouldn't take back the months he lay at death's door because God used his experience to help him more compassionately minister comfort to others.

The Psalms show David expressing fear and frustration to God, yet proclaiming hope in God's character and faithfulness.

God reigns. He loves us. He is writing and redeeming history through the story of our lives. In the moments when you fear, remember that even your fears are part of God's greater plan.

Dear Father, my instinct is to run from my fears. Yet You want to change me as I respond to them by trusting You. Help me to gain wisdom and trust You more as I face my fears. Help me to grow in discernment and godliness so that I can better love others and love You. Teach me to step forward in my moments of fear, rather than to step away. Amen.

1. Dave had always enjoyed good health and feared what it would be like if he ever became sick. What do you fear? How do you deal with those fears?

2. How does God's Word provide comfort for you in your times of fear?

ATTITUDE

For as [a man] thinks within himself, so he is.

PROVERBS 23:7 (NASB)

Oxygen deprivation damaged Rick Hoyt's brain at birth. He was born with cerebral palsy and spastic quadriplegia. His parents, Dick and Judy, were told Rick would never lead a "normal" life and were encouraged to institutionalize him.

Rick couldn't walk or speak, but he learned to communicate by moving his eyes. His parents discovered he was a bright child who could learn like other children. When Rick was twelve years old, the engineering team at Tufts University created a computer called the Hope Machine that helps Rick communicate. In spite of doctors' negative prognoses, Rick graduated from high school and completed a bachelor's degree from Boston University. Today he lives independently in his own apartment.

While he was in high school, Rick learned about a five-mile charity road race to raise funds for a paralyzed teenager. He asked his father if he would be willing to help him compete. With that first competition, Team Hoyt's racing career began. In 2011, Rick and his father completed their thousandth event with the running of the Boston Marathon. In the past thirty years, they've competed in over 240 triathlons and 68 marathons, with Dick's fastest time just thirty minutes off the world's record time.

Rick Hoyt believes in the power of attitude. He may have limitations, but God has gifted him with strengths and abilities, and he's chosen to focus on those abilities. Team Hoyt's slogan is *Yes You Can!*, and the father and son believe the attitudes they've chosen led to the choices they made and the success they found, both in Rick's education and their sports endeavors. They believe that what's crucial is not what happens to us in life but what happens in us and through us as a result.

The father-son team beautifully exemplifies the sacrificial love our heavenly Father pours out on our behalf. For example, records demonstrate that Dick actually runs faster when he's pushing his one-hundred-and-ten-pound son than when he's running on his own. His love drives him to dig deeper, yet Dick claims his son's spirit is the force behind the team's success.

"When I run, I feel like my disability disappears," Rick states. As a father, Dick's driving passion is to give his son moments of freedom that transcend the limitations of his body. This passion has driven Dick to pull, carry, and push Rick through each leg of the 2.4-mile swim, 112-mile bike, and 26.2-mile run in each of the six Ironman events the father-son team has completed. No surprise that in 2008, Team Hoyt was inducted into the Ironman Hall of Fame in Hawaii.

Because God created us in His image, our hearts resonate when we hear about heroes like Dick and Rick Hoyt, who reflect the same sacrificial attitudes as God himself and Jesus Christ. As children of God, we were created to reflect hope, determination, and a persevering spirit. Those attributes are rooted in the character of God and His Son Jesus Christ, who desire a personal relationship with each one of us. No matter how positive our attitude, we cannot find ultimate fulfillment apart from Jesus. The starting place as we evaluate our attitudes toward success in life is to evaluate our relationship with our Creator God. Do you know Him?

Father, give me eyes to see past the circumstances to the hope beyond. Help me to believe that what's crucial is not what happens to me in life but what happens in me and through me through the power of Your Spirit. Help me bring cups of cold water to those around me and to show them the hope that is in You alone. Amen.

1. How has the power of attitude influenced your life? What results have you seen?

2. How does hope influence the decisions you make for the future?

ANGER

Cease from anger and forsake wrath; Do not fret; it leads only to evildoing.
PSALM 37:8 (NASB)

Not a day passes without Chris vividly remembering the moment a one-ton steel plate slipped from the rigging that was moving the slab of metal from one machine to another in the shop where he worked. In one second that forever changed his life, his body was crushed from the neck down.

Chris thought he was alone in the building, except for his supervisor, who was in the office and too far from Chris to hear his voice. Still, he called out for help and prayed someone would hear him as he struggled against the enveloping blackness. Each breath was agony as he fought to remain conscious. Providentially, a co-worker who had come to work early heard Chris' faint cries and called 9-1-1. As they waited for medical help to arrive, workers used a forklift to free Chris's crushed body.

Chris was taken by helicopter to UC Davis Medical Center in Sacramento, where it was discovered that the metal plate had crushed the nerves in his body, his pelvis, and his hips. His bladder, spleen, kidneys, and liver had also been severely damaged. He was placed on dialysis and told he would remain on it for the rest of his life. He was also told it was unlikely he would ever walk again.

Although Chris was glad to be alive, he was angry—at himself. He'd taken pride in being the best possible worker for his employer. He'd worked for years to receive his journeyman's license as a machinist, just completed a three-month probation period at his job, and received a raise. He'd worked long and hard to find a job he loved that would support his family. The future he'd worked so hard to secure for his family seemed gone, and he felt responsible.

Long weeks in the hospital gave Chris the opportunity to spend time in prayer talking to God. He'd spent years playing games with God—living life by his own rules, thinking he could ask for forgiveness any time he wanted. But his stay in the hospital changed that.

"God stopped me and said, 'You're not running any more.' Before my accident, I was a believer but not a follower of Christ. God was giving me a chance to discover what it was like to have Jesus living inside me. I never experienced that until after my accident."

Over the months of his recovery, God used Chris's difficult circumstances to change his spiritual priorities and his relationships within his family. His wife, Elaine, came to know Jesus personally as a result of Chris's accident.

"I see that God used what happened to me to bring me and my family back to Him. I'm so thankful for that. I have so much to be grateful for. Doctors said I'd never walk, but today I'm using a cane. They said I'd be on dialysis the rest of my life, but they were wrong. God took my legs, but He gave them back and showed me what it was like to walk with Him.

"I still struggle with anger at myself sometimes. But I can't waste my time being angry at myself when I understand that God isn't angry at me. He has things for me to do, and my anger just gets in the way."

What about you? Are you struggling with anger? If so, pray about how anger might be wasting your time and keeping you from doing the things God has in store for you.

Dear Father, I'm tempted to become angry at myself, at others, and at You when I experience pain and disappointment. Help me to understand that You work to bring good into my life in spite of the tragedies and losses that I see around me. You are a God of mercy who stands ready to heal and to comfort in my moments of pain. Help me to forgive myself as You have forgiven me and to extend Your forgiveness and grace to others. Amen.

1. Do you feel angry at yourself for falling short or for acting in a manner you feel has hurt those you love? Do you have difficulty forgiving yourself? What do you think Jesus would say to you?

2. How does anger "get in the way" in your life?

DEATH OF DREAMS

Those who hope in the Lord will renew their strength. They will soar on wings like eagles; they will run and not grow weary, they will walk and not be faint.

ISAIAH 40:31

I n 1995 at the age of thirty-three, Kate Adamson was living the American dream. A native New Zealander, she lived in a Southern California beach town with her devoted husband, Steven, and two beautiful daughters. She exercised and watched what she ate, and she was preparing to launch a personal training business. Life was good.

So Kate didn't give it much thought when one day she felt strangely dizzy. Within a short time, she was struggling to think, speak, or move. Her husband raced her to the hospital, and before long, she was terrified to find herself totally paralyzed.

Doctors assumed Kate could feel and hear nothing, so they worked on her without administering painkillers. Unfortunately, she felt excruciating pain during each medical procedure and tried, unsuccessfully, to scream out to those around her.

As Kate listened to the doctors discussing their findings, she learned she'd experienced a double brain stem stroke, a medical crisis so severe that few people survive. She wasn't expected to breathe without assistance, walk again, or live. Doctors encouraged her husband, a lawyer, to remove her feeding tube and allow her to "die with dignity." But Steven refused and fought tirelessly for her life.

Kate eventually showed those around her that she could communicate by blinking—her only source of movement. Doctors finally realized she felt pain, and they were overwhelmed to learn her mental capacities were intact. Over the ensuing months and years, Kate fought to learn to walk again with a cane, to dress herself (although movement on her left side remains limited), and to perform tasks most of us take for granted.

Kate's dream of launching a personal training business and the health she'd always known had disappeared. What kept her from sinking into bitterness and moved her to become a motivational speaker who travels the world inspiring others?

"Before my stroke, my life was fear-driven. I ran from hard things," Kate says. "My stroke forced me to find inner strength. God was the only person I could talk to. Every time I experienced fear, I turned my fear into faith. I used Scripture to transform negative thoughts into positive truth by telling myself God would give me strength to do what I needed to do each minute and each hour."

Kate had the support of family and friends in her struggle: "I was blessed to have people surrounding me who read to me from the Bible. I also relied on worship music."

But Kate admits that pushing through her recovery was tough. "I've never prayed so much in my life. My stroke was the most frightening thing I'd ever been through, and I had to fight this fight on my own. Sometimes I wanted to turn my brain off, but the Word was my comfort. I had no idea God had a bigger purpose for me, that He was going to use me to become a voice for the voiceless to speak on behalf of brain stem injury survivors. God uses us for purposes far beyond our understanding. He put us here to make a difference in other people's lives."

Kate offers encouragement to others who've experienced stroke, medical trauma, or devastating loss: "Find others who are going through your experience who can offer hope. Never give up hope. Isaiah 40:31 tells us that those who hope in the Lord will renew their strength. We hold on to that truth because we place our hope in a loving, faithful God who gave His own Son for us because He loved us so much. I can trust a God who loves me that much with even the worst circumstances of my life."

> *Dear God, sometimes it's hard for me to believe that You have dreams for me. But I will choose to believe Your Word—that You've called me to a hope and a future. Help me to believe You are a God of miracles, but to lay down a demanding spirit that thinks You owe me. Thank You for the opportunities of this day and this hour, and may I have a heart willing to invest all I have for You. Amen.*

1. Have you ever had to let go of a dream? How did you handle it?

2. What does it mean for you to fight through your pain alone, yet still rely upon God?

Trials, Temptations, and Triumph

Though Satan should buffet, though trials should come,
Let this blessed assurance control . . .

God is God. Because He is God, He is worthy of my trust and obedience.
I will find rest nowhere but in His holy will, a will that is unspeakably beyond
my largest notions of what He is up to.

ELISABETH ELLIOT

If we're honest, we would probably have to admit we've had moments when we've thought the promises in the Bible were written for someone else. It can be tough to lean back into God's arms in total trust when we've just been handed a cancer diagnosis, been denied by an insurance carrier, or been told we're about to lose a foot to diabetes. It seems some days crises fly at us like snowflakes in a blizzard. In moments of pain and suffering, we live in the tension of who we believe God to be and who He appears to be if we use circumstances to define Him.

One privilege of living in the twenty-first century is being able to look back at the lives of people in the Bible. We can learn much from one biblical figure, Joseph, who faced the reality of suffering in his life. He believed God was good and loving, yet circumstances seemed to indicate the opposite. One after another, the good things in Joseph's life were stripped away: his freedom, his reputation, his family, the comforts of home. He was wrongly accused and confined while evil men ran free. He was imprisoned while injustice prevailed. He lived for years with no visible evidence that God was working out things "for his good." Yet Joseph held firmly to faith in a loving God.

Why?

Joseph's faith was rooted in his commitment to truth, not in what he could see. He believed in a trustworthy God who kept His word and fulfilled His promises and covenants (Psalm 105:1–11). He believed God's faithfulness was greater than his circumstances suggested (Psalm 105:8). He believed God sovereignly intervened in the course of human lives and history; therefore, he trusted God with his own circumstances (Psalm 105:12–15). He believed God guarded him from the full weight of this world's evil and protected him from what he could not see (Psalm 105:14–15, 17). And Joseph acted, based upon what he believed. He applied what he knew; he made choices that demonstrated he was preparing for the future God had promised him (Genesis 37:1–11).

Joseph—like us—lived much of his life in the tension of disparity; his experiences didn't seem to match up with the promises God had made him. Yet he clung unswervingly to his faith. Like Horatio Spafford, he didn't allow circumstances to alter his beliefs or dictate his choices.

Trials and hardships are a certainty of life, but they don't have the power to control us or shape our future when our faith rests in the character of a trustworthy God who has proven himself and who promises that through His Son Jesus Christ, we, too, will triumph in all things.

CHRONIC PAIN

It was good for me to be afflicted so that I might learn your decrees.

PSALM 119:71

W endy Wallace's chest pains couldn't have come at a more in-convenient time. She was leading an out-of-town corporate training when she assumed she was having a reaction to a new allergy medication. She took antacids and waited. But her pain escalated and hours later her training partner insisted on driving her to the emergency room.

At the ER, doctors hesitated to admit her. Wendy was forty-seven, of average weight, a nonsmoker who didn't drink, a conscientious and healthy eater, and physically fit. Thankfully, her business partner insisted she be evaluated, and doctors discovered that 30 percent of her heart had been damaged by a heart attack. The next day Wendy flew home to Michigan. Less than twenty-four hours later, she suffered a second heart attack, followed by an allergic reaction to dye used to illuminate her arteries during a catheterization procedure. The medical team soon recognized her heart attacks had been caused by vasculitis, a complication of recently diagnosed lupus.

Even though she'd been sick since she was a teenager, Wendy's stoic family had taught her to ignore the puzzling array of symptoms that plagued her into her adult years: fainting spells, fevers, exhaustion, relentless joint and muscle pain. Her lupus diagnosis brought relief and treatment, but not an end to her illnesses. Doctors soon discovered that her gallbladder was diseased, and she was also diagnosed with large cell lung cancer, which required the removal of a lung and painful rehab. Months later, doctors also removed a tumor and eighteen inches of Wendy's colon. As she was wheeled to the car to return home, she experienced a third heart attack. In the two years that followed, she was diagnosed with debilitating arthritis and more than twenty other painful diseases.

How does Wendy live with constant pain and physical loss? She admits that at first she was angry at doctors' incompetence and mismanagement, but she's learned to extend God's grace and forgiveness. She also reminds herself that nothing happens to her that is beyond God's control. She rests securely in God's hands, no matter her circumstances, and she believes pain is her opportunity to become more like Jesus.

Wendy also believes that pain and illness are part of God's assignment for her. She uses her influence as a speaker and the author of *Doing Well at Being Sick* and draws from her professional background to encourage others who live with chronic illness.

In her book, she writes, "God often allows us to stew . . . until we are ready to accept the fact that He has been in control all of the time. All along He has been much more interested in my spiritual growth than in my physical healing. I have had a great deal to learn, and He took the time to teach me because of his deep love for me."

In spite of chronic pain, Wendy is committed to reflecting gratitude each day, finding joy in every circumstance, and serving those around her, rather than focusing on herself. She truly believes that it is worth being afflicted to draw closer to God and to become more like Jesus Christ.

Do you also desire to learn more about God in the "teaching moments" of your pain?

Father, in spite of my pain, help me reflect an attitude of gratitude and find joy in my circumstances. Give me the heart of a servant toward those around me. Let me see that You have placed me here to glorify You by blessing others as I become more like Your Son Jesus. Amen.

1. Have you struggled to "do well at being sick"? In what ways?

2. Do you view your illness as part of God's "assignment" for you?

STANDING FIRM

If you do not stand firm in your faith, you will not stand at all.

ISAIAH 7:9

Recently I was asked to speak at the Central California Women's Facility in Chowchilla, California, the largest women's prison in the world. The morning I was scheduled to speak, my ministry partner and I left our hotel, allowing what we thought to be more than adequate travel time. However, thirty minutes into our journey, it became clear we'd taken a wrong turn. The prison is located in a remote agricultural area that resembles a scene from a sci-fi movie, and somewhere along our route, I'd zigged when I should have zagged. Unfortunately, I hadn't been given a street address for the prison, and as I wandered through fields of almond groves, I longed for the familiar voice of my GPS. After all, most of us like the reassurance of knowing we're headed in the right direction.

Over the past dozen years, I've faced a maze of relational, emotional, physical, and spiritual choices, some as part of life in general and some as a result of living with uncertain health. I've often wondered which way to turn, praying I could hear God's voice telling me the "right" thing to do. But over the years I've found that turning to God to serve as my "spiritual GPS" shortchanges the process of heart-change I so often need as I seek God in prayer. In my seeking, turning, and even moments of desperation, I develop greater dependency upon God's sufficiency. I experience growth I would never have known if God had simply pointed me down a one-way street.

We live in a challenging and changing world, and as a result we desire direction and black-and-white answers to tough problems. Yet God's Word never promises easy lives or easy answers for problems. Instead it promises that problems are an invitation to an intimate relationship with God himself, a God whose love and character never waver in an ever-changing world.

Twenty-two times in Scripture believers are encouraged to "stand fast" in challenging times. The phrase "stand fast" most often refers to the quality of our faith, not the method we use to make decisions. What makes it possible for us to stand fast in our faith, in spite of setbacks and slipups, discouragement and disappointment, challenges and changes?

- *A righteous, loving God chooses to be in relationship with us* (Ephesians 1:3–4). God chose us and blesses us. His greatest desire is to share a relationship with us.
- *God rejoices in doing good for us* (Zephaniah 3:14–17). God saved us and took our punishment; He delights and rejoices in us.
- *God works out even the painful circumstances in our lives for our good* (Romans 8:28). God is not limited by our circumstances and works in all things for our good.
- *God will meet all our needs so we can overflow with good works* (2 Corinthians 9:8). God chooses to bless us not only because He loves us, but so we can bless others out of the overflow of our blessings.

• *God promises that if He looks after the sparrows, He'll certainly take care of us* (Luke 12:6–7). God is interested in every detail of our lives and cares for us in countless ways we may be unaware of.

What direction do you need in your life today? Stand firm in the confidence that God's love is unshakable, and He rejoices in doing good for you.

Dear God, so much about my life is uncertain, and no matter how much I plan, I can never be sure what tomorrow may hold. The only certainty in life is Your character, Your unfailing love, and Your unchanging Word. May I commit each day to standing on the unchanging truth of Your Word and to growing in my relationship with You, the only measure of success in this life and in eternity. Amen.

1. When has God unexpectedly met your needs?

2. Pray through the list above as you ask God to show you more of His great heart for you.

Denial

Do not merely listen to the word, and so deceive yourselves. Do what it says. Anyone who listens to the word but does not do what it says is like a man who looks at his face in a mirror and, after looking at himself, goes away and immediately forgets what he looks like. But the man who looks intently into the perfect law that gives freedom, and continues to do this, not forgetting what he has heard, but doing it—he will be blessed in what he does.

JAMES 1:22–25

The canes have been leaning in a corner of the bedroom for more than a year, strategically placed in a location my husband must pass at least a half dozen times a day. In the sixteen months since I placed them there, they've gone untouched, though not unnoticed. I have mastered the art of gently bringing them to Dan's attention with a flicker of my eyes, a nod of my head, or a casual comment. His response is always the same: a tolerant smile that masks the stubborn denial that lies beneath.

For the past eight years, Dan has lived with a condition called peripheral neuropathy. The disease has caused the degeneration of the nervous system in his feet, legs, and hands, compromising his balance and ability to feel and manipulate his feet, as well as his fingers.

Because he can't feel his feet, he can't feel inclines, slopes, pebbles, irregularities, or surface changes beneath his feet. Dan walks using his eyes to gauge distance and dangers, and his hands and arms help him retain balance. In the past two years, he's taken several tumbles, one resulting in a torn rotator cuff, surgery, and painful rehab.

But Dan doesn't need a cane. Just ask him.

Even though his orthopedist recommends a cane. And his neurologist. And his rehab specialist. But who's keeping track? (Perhaps me. I'm sure keeping track of Dan's stuff was written into our marriage vows somewhere . . .)

Experts tell us that denial is based in fear and our inability to face the truth. Denial gives us an illusion of safety and security. We create our own reality: Rules that apply to other people don't apply to us. We're not accountable. Denial becomes a dark closet where we tuck away painful truth we're unwilling to face. Unfortunately, when we hide things, they can rot, stink, and become more troublesome.

We easily slip into patterns of denial about habits, attitudes, and unbiblical lifestyles. We're all guilty. For years I waved my victim mentality like a banner yet denied I possessed it.

How do we avoid the trap of denial? The only sure way to protect ourselves is to saturate our thinking with the Word of God, to submit ourselves to the conviction of the Spirit of God, and to remain accountable to the people of God.

Today, after two weeks on his back following painful eye surgery, Dan picked up a cane as he headed out the door to go back to work. He plans to use it for just a few days, he told me. How long he uses it will be up to him, but picking it up was a start, and I'm proud of him.

Father, give me a heart willing to admit my fears and failures. Show me the blind spots in my character. Give me a heart willing to obey Your Word and to submit to Your Spirit. Amen.

1. What about your circumstances, health, future, diagnosis, prognosis, etc., do you tend to deny? How does this affect your relationships with others and your spiritual, emotional, and physical health?

2. How have you dealt with your blind spots and your areas of denial? What tools have you used? What truth do you think God wants you to understand about these areas of your life?

Every Single Tear

You keep track of all my sorrows. You have collected all my tears in your bottle.
You have recorded each one in your book.

PSALM 56:8 (NLT)

Jessica is our only daughter and the love of her father's life. She was born with an adventurer's heart. After graduating from high school, she went to college and earned a degree in radio broadcasting, but her passion has always been working in orphanages. By the time she was twenty, she'd lived in several countries, trained in natural disaster work, and responded in the first wave of relief after the most powerful tsunami in history decimated parts of Indonesia in December of 2006.

As a proud father, Dan dreamed of the day he'd walk Jessica down the aisle. In the fall of 2011, we received her excited call. Could we fly from Michigan to Seattle in four weeks for her wedding to her Jamaican fiancé, Mosiah?

We knew Mosiah's visa status meant we'd have limited time to prepare for the wedding, and the race was on. I made arrangements to surprise Jessica by flying out for the wedding a few days early. Dan would follow two days later. The day before Dan's departure, the retina in his left eye detached. He needed emergency surgery to save his vision. His doctor made the choices clear: Dan could risk his vision by delaying the surgery or miss his daughter's wedding.

Blindness wasn't an option, and Dan was devastated. His father's heart was broken. To make matters worse, our entire family had already flown to Washington. Not a single family member remained in Michigan to be with him during his surgery or to care for him during a recovery that forced him to lie still on his back for two weeks.

As he lay on the couch in the home of friends, questions filled his mind. Why hadn't God allowed him just a few more days—time enough to get to the wedding and back? Why had he been left alone at home? Why did Jessica's heart have to be broken? Why had he not been given the chance to spend time with his new son-in-law?

Dan didn't have the answers to those questions, but he did have the answers to two, more important questions.

Could he trust God for the bigger picture? Yes.

Was it necessary for him to understand? No.

Dan and I had taught our children to trust God for the bigger picture—to look beyond the suffering in orphanages and from tsunamis to a sovereign God who promises purpose and meaning. We'd taught Jessica that suffering is to be expected; we are not immune from the pain of life. And we will not always have easy answers.

My husband lay on a couch on the day of our daughter's wedding and was grateful for Skype technology that allowed him to see her face, talk to her, and share in her wedding ceremony. Our family watched as he wept tears of a father with a broken heart. But I believe God wept with Dan that day, knowing the pain of his father's heart, separated from his child.

Scripture tells us that God collects our tears. Perhaps one day in heaven, our Father will return them as a precious gift of love.

Dear Father, give me faith to trust You in those moments when it feels as though life has "cheated" me. Thank You for loving me so much that my tears move Your heart. Thank You for a love that defies my comprehension. Amen.

1. What tears do you believe God may have collected for you?

2. We are not promised immunity from the pain of life. Have you ever been frustrated with God, believing He should protect you from circumstances? How has this influenced your walk of faith?

When Life Seems Unfair

May the groans of the prisoners come before you; by the strength of your arm preserve those condemned to die . . . Then we your people, the sheep of your pasture, will praise you forever; from generation to generation we will recount your praise.

PSALM 79:11, 13

When doctors released me from the hospital in 1999 to return home and recover from my brain lesion, they cautioned me: "Your health is fragile, Shelly. Over the next few years, it will be important to rest and guard against stress."

Rest? Guard against stress? Fast-forward a year, and stress was sweeping through my life like a horde of bargain shoppers on Black Friday. Dan had taken a new job that required us to move across the country. Our prodigal son had returned home, and our daughter had moved home after six months of tsunami relief work with symptoms of post-traumatic stress disorder. To make life even more exciting, my father-in-law with Parkinson's disease and a half dozen other medical diagnoses had moved in with us, and Dan and I had taken on the care of my father and mother with Alzheimer's, three states away.

Long-distance caregiving exhausted me. After four years of racing back and forth between states, Dan and I returned to Michigan, bringing his father, Norman, with us and leaving our struggling adult children behind. We soon moved Norman to the veterans' home four miles from us and moved my mother with Alzheimer's and father into our home. I was caring for three parents and managing their medical appointments while I juggled book deadlines, SOS calls from the kids, and, when I could fit it in, occasional pseudo housecleaning to help ease my guilt. In light of what the doctors had told me, my life just didn't seem . . . fair.

As our parents' conditions deteriorated, my stress increased. At least twice a year, I was scurried to the emergency room with symptoms eerily similar to those that nearly took my life in 1999. But what could I do? Where was I supposed to find the time to care for myself? Often the most difficult thing I did was step over the threshold of my own home as I struggled to hold back my tide of frustrations. And some days, those frustrations boiled over into anger.

I'd always thought that anger was a sin. But a counselor shared with me that anger is a natural, God-given emotion. Psalm 79 teaches key principles of constructive anger management. In our anger, we should strive to:

+ *Direct our anger at the right source.* We must remember that God is not the source of evil in our lives (vv. 1–3). He's the source of all comfort, righteousness, and healing.
+ *Acknowledge God as righteous and holy.* God is merciful and loving, but He directs His anger at those who refuse to acknowledge His sovereignty in His world (vv. 4–7).
+ *Throw ourselves on the mercy of God and glorify His name.* When we acknowledge God in the most desperate moments of our lives, we worship and glorify His name (vv. 9–10).

• *Freely express our "groans" to God.* God listens to our cries of suffering (v. 11). His heart is moved because of His great love for us.
• *Acknowledge God as "good," in even our most painful moments.* Even as we groan in our suffering, we can still express God's goodness. His strength preserves us, and He battles on our behalf.

During my caregiving years, I learned to explore the reasons and sources of my anger and submit them to God. As I prayed for wisdom for the most appropriate ways to deal with my frustrations, God often showed me just what needed tweaking in my heart and my attitude. In the process, I learned that my anger could become a path to forgiveness and growth.

Father, sometimes I feel angry and overwhelmed, but You're with me in those moments. You know my pain and frustration. Today I bring my groans to You. Thank You for Your great compassion and love for me, for Your heart that is moved to act with compassion and mercy. I choose to praise You even now. Amen.

1. When have you struggled with anger? How did you handle it?

2. What "groans" can you express to God in this moment of your life?

Not What I Signed Up For

*I am still confident of this: I will see the goodness of the Lord
in the land of the living.*

PSALM 27:13

Therisse grew up with dreams of having a fairy-tale life. She believed a husband would one day ride into her life, sweep her off
her feet, and carry her off to his castle, where he'd pamper her and
protect her from the world. And when she married Noel—a tall,
dark, handsome Central American with a rich accent—Therisse believed her prince had come.

For a few years the story held its glimmer. Yet the greatest threat
to her fairy tale came not from the outside world like a typical story,
but from the things Therisse and Noel carried within themselves.
Even Noel's powers of protection couldn't defeat his wife's struggle
with chronic illness. Children came, and with them, heartbreaks.
Noel and Therisse fought, and at times it seemed the promise of
"happily ever after" vanished forever.

Even though Therisse's fairy-tale life was filled with heartache
and loss, the prince and princess stayed together. Life would be different, perhaps, after retirement, she dreamed again. They could

slow down and focus on each other, spend more time together, perhaps begin again at creating the fairy tale Therisse had envisioned.

But only two months after Noel's retirement, doctors diagnosed him with Parkinson's disease. The couple didn't panic. Noel wasn't desperately ill; they could handle what was ahead. And they were right—for a time. For a time following Noel's diagnosis, life seemed somewhat "normal."

Three years later, Therisse faced the truth: the princess was now a caregiver. Her crown was askew and her prince had tumbled from his horse. It had become her job to maintain his dignity and care for him. She could choose it willingly or grudgingly. Or she could walk away and search for another prince.

Therisse chose to stay. She packed up their belongings and moved them to a tiny one-bedroom apartment that would better accommodate their financial situation and the dangers of Noel's frequent falls. Today Noel requires round-the-clock care. He never complains, and in that sense, he is truly a prince.

In the past months, Noel's needs have escalated. He had a stroke that weakened him further and required him to move into a nursing home for rehabilitation and an operation to replace his pacemaker battery. Therisse spends long hours with him every day, overseeing his care. His mobility has diminished, and it's increasingly difficult for him to swallow. But even when his health was at its worst, Noel prayed and ministered to those who cared for him.

Therisse admits she's tired. She admits she's faced discouragement and loneliness. But it's been in the difficult months since Noel's stroke that the "ever after" has settled into her spirit as she's watched her husband fight some of his most valiant battles for his Lord from a wheelchair. She stands faithfully beside him, a princess with a crown slightly askew, but faithfully loving him and cheering him on to the end.

Father, today may my prayer be "Thy will be done," in spite of the challenges that lie before me. Life does not look like a fairy tale, and reality is staring me in the face. Help me to submit my will and my attitude to You, moment by moment. Amen.

1. At some point in your life, did your "fairy tale" change into cold, harsh reality? How did you handle those circumstances?

2. Is God calling you to a new "ever after" in some area of your life? If so, where, and what may be required of you?

Beauty beyond the Scars

Provide for those who grieve in Zion—to bestow on them a crown of beauty instead of ashes, the oil of gladness instead of mourning, and a garment of praise instead of a spirit of despair. They will be called oaks of righteousness, a planting of the Lord for the display of his splendor.

Isaiah 61:3

Twenty-six year-old Ann didn't like the words *ulcerative colitis* or *surgery*, so she left her doctor's office and spent six months pretending she wasn't desperately ill. After all, for most of her life, she hadn't even known what it felt like to be sick, and she told herself she could beat this disease. She clung to the lie until the colitis ate away her insides, causing blood poisoning that landed her in the emergency room.

This time, Ann couldn't escape the stark realities of her illness. An ileostomy was her only option if she hoped to live. When she awoke in intensive care, surgeons had removed her large intestine and her rectum. The ileostomy created a surgical opening that brought Ann's small intestine out through the wall of her stomach above the groin, where her body wastes would be eliminated.

Ann was suddenly faced with the challenge of learning how to feel feminine wearing her body waste strapped to her abdomen.

"I was a size seven, and feeling attractive had always been important to me. Suddenly, I had to figure out how to feel beautiful and sexy with my poop sitting on a scar on my belly."

Ann had a hundred questions: Could the bag leak or break? Would it smell? Would she be able to wear a bathing suit? What about sex? Beyond her questions, she had to choose her attitude—had God robbed her of her beauty, femininity, and freedom in intimacy?

Admittedly, Ann hadn't cared much about God before her surgery. She was living life on her own terms. Her brother had committed suicide, and she'd slid into depression. She and her husband had separated. Then the surgery left her in excruciating pain.

She says, "I was given a fifty percent chance of survival the day doctors cut me open. It was hard waking up with that bag. I went through a mourning period. But looking death in the face made me think about hard things.

"Four years later I surrendered my life to Jesus. He gave me a speaking and teaching ministry. He saved me from a future that most certainly would have centered on me. God began to teach me what it meant to give myself to Him—body and soul."

Ann's lessons would stretch over a lifetime as she negotiated a new sense of contentment with her changed body. She learned to laugh at herself and developed an openness about her condition that put others at ease.

"Jesus gave up perfection for us. He willingly took on dandruff, body odor . . . maybe He even had ingrown toenails. We know His human body wasn't perfect because it was human. When I took on scars and imperfection, I became a little more like Him."

Ann never lost her love of beauty or her vibrant attractiveness.

Today she cares for her new husband, whose body is failing. She knows what it's like to watch what was once taken for granted slip away. And while she's grieved for her losses, she also thanks God for using her pain as His intervention to draw her to Him.

Dear Father, Your precious Son Jesus chose scars for me. He chose disfigurement and the pains and limitations of a physical body. Thank You for His sacrifice on my behalf. Help me remember that I am beautiful because Your beauty is bestowed on me as Your image-bearer. Thank You that even my pain can be a tool in Your hands to make me more like Your Son. Amen.

1. We live in a society with a high standard of beauty. In what ways can we glorify God through illnesses and procedures that alter us physically?

2. How can we choose to put on a "garment of praise" for a "spirit of despair" (Isaiah 61:3)?

His Eye Is on the Sparrow

Are not five sparrows sold for two pennies? Yet not one of them is forgotten by God.

LUKE 12:6

E very morning I sit at my computer to work and eventually end up watching the birds that come to the three feeders outside my front window. I make up stories about their imaginary families and relationships as I watch them hover and flit from branch to branch and feeder to feeder. The amiable finches often sit in twosomes on their perches, munching away as they swing in the breeze. The brilliant cardinals and bluejays sometimes duke it out for priority status at the biggest feeder, with the bluejays typically winning. And the grackles take over like bullies, sending everyone scattering when they descend like Al Capone's mob.

I identify most with the sparrows, who live in the spruce bushes that line our front sidewalk. These bushes transform into a noisy, snow-encrusted sparrow apartment complex in winter. During the morning and afternoon hours, sparrows pop through openings in the branches, chattering and surveying the yard. Then, as if someone fired a starting gun for a race, they rush the feeders en masse, where they chow down together like Baptists at a church potluck.

How interesting that God has chosen to comfort us by comparing us to sparrows, the most insignificant and vulnerable of birds. Sparrows depend so much upon companionship that a lone sparrow is considered a symbol of loneliness. In biblical times, their dirty nests were considered unclean, yet they were allowed to remain undisturbed under the temple eaves (Psalm 84:3). The poorest of the poor offered sparrows for sacrifices in the temple because they could be bought so cheaply (Leviticus 14:1–7). Two could be purchased for about a quarter in today's currency, and if you bought four, an extra bird was often thrown in for free (Luke 12:6–7).

Yet God chose the sparrow to show us that His love for us is intimate beyond our comprehension. If He cares about the welfare of the most insignificant of birds, imagine how much He cares for us. Nothing about us escapes God's loving notice, not our heartaches, fears, worries, or the smallest annoyances of daily life. His watchfulness over the sparrows gives us three assurances.

- *God's sovereignty extends to things we often see as "insignificant."* Even the smallest details in God's creation are important to Him. He cares about each concern that moves our heart.
- *God is compassionate.* If He cares enough to notice the suffering of a single bird in the vastness of His creation, how much does He care about us?
- *God doesn't forget us.* In the moments when we feel insignificant and forgotten, we can know we are loved by a God who knows when each bird falls to the ground.

Do you feel discouraged? Remember that the sparrows are God's reminder of His unfailing love and care for you.

Dear Father, when I feel discouraged and lonely, help me remember that Jesus is my friend. If His eye is on the sparrow, I can know He watches me. Take away my doubt and fear, and help me rest in Your goodness. When I'm tempted and hope dies, may I draw closer to You, knowing You care for me. Amen.

1. Read through the words of the hymn "His Eye Is on the Sparrow." How do the words comfort you regarding God's intimate love for you?

2. Even the sparrows fall. God doesn't promise that His loved ones won't experience difficult times. Meditate on Psalm 84:3 as God's message to your heart.

Relentless Joy

Praise the Lord, O my soul, and forget not all his benefits . . . who redeems your life from the pit and crowns you with love and compassion.

PSALM 103:2, 4

I lie in bed facing the shadows on the ceiling cast by the night-light and listen for the creaking of the door across the hallway. I whisper the prayer I've prayed each night for more than two years—that my mother will sleep.

Even as my heart voices the words, I know time is running out. In minutes, the skewed circadian rhythms of my mother's body will wake her, and her nightly wandering will begin—the circuit from the kitchen to the living room, down the hall and back to the kitchen.

I squeeze my eyes shut and will the burning muscles in my calves to relax, but they refuse. Pain rips through my feet and legs, and I jerk to a seated position. This is my nightly dance. Moments after I lie down, peripheral neuropathy shoots searing pain through my toes, feet, and legs. Could life be more ironic? Even my tiniest snippets of rest are stalked by pain.

I hear my mother stir in her room, and I rise and meet her in the hallway. Her frame is thin beneath her pink nightgown, and she is whimpering.

She wants to go home.

I walk beside her and we talk, of her childhood home on the corner of Getty Street, of her mother and sister, Erma, and brothers Eddie and Elwin. I steer her for the umpteenth time away from the dangers of the stairwell. Like the night before and nights before that, I've slept just minutes after a day of writing, laundry, cooking, cleaning, and doctors' appointments. Each day I diverted her from countless perils: quarters and dimes on the counter (who'd have thought they were snack food?), throw rugs (trip-and-fall), and unlocked doors (the Great Escape).

A migraine pounds behind my eyes and a fog clouds my brain, but I will myself to stay awake. I guide my mother to the living room couch where we settle and turn our attention to reruns of *I Love Lucy*. Pain shoots up my leg as scenes flicker across the television screen. My mind drifts, and images roll through my memory: Dan silhouetted in a chair beside me in the dim light of my hospital room. The brush of his hand against my face as he spoons droplets of applesauce into my mouth. His hand stroking my arm in the darkness.

I look at my mother beside me through my migraine fog as pain surges through my leg, and I choose joy. Not happiness, but the living, breathing truth that God's great and glorious plan surpasses all I see or understand.

I choose joy for the moment. Joy for the gift of presence. Joy for reassurance of purpose in pain. Joy for the blessings of memory. Joy for the gift of mystery that calls us to God in our suffering. Joy for promised healing beyond the boundaries of earthly time. Joy for the promise that God's bigger picture surpasses our understanding.

And I pray for a relentless joy sustained by the hope of Jesus Christ that will strengthen me for the road ahead.

Father, sometimes I expect joy to come as an emotion. Instead, help me to see it as a choice and a mind-set. Today I choose joy in my circumstances, Father. You have chosen me and redeemed me, crowned me with love and compassion, and I can do nothing less than overflow with joy at Your great love for me, for those I love, and for a broken world. Amen.

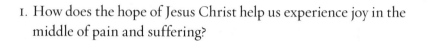

1. How does the hope of Jesus Christ help us experience joy in the middle of pain and suffering?

2. When have you chosen joy as a conscious act?

Reputation

A good name is more desirable than great riches;
to be esteemed is better than silver or gold.

Proverbs 22:1

Larry has been confined to a wheelchair for chronic back pain
and partial paralysis for more than three years, yet his medical condition has gone undiagnosed. He finds himself continually
struggling to convince his medical provider that his pain is real and
his needs are worthy of their attention. Because his condition is
undiagnosed, workers' compensation has denied his applications.
Larry's life consists of long hours on the phone with people who
seem skeptical about his condition and reluctant to help in any way.

Larry admits that some days he feels like screaming at people on
the other end of the phone. But in those moments he reminds himself that his pain is his calling to interact with people who are trying
to support themselves by making calls to frustrated, angry people.
In those moments, Larry reminds himself that his job is to show
people Jesus' love, no matter his frustration.

Sue was diagnosed with a brain tumor ten years ago. Surgery to
remove her mass was successful, but a doctor's error following the

surgery left her with speech and swallowing difficulties. It's hard for her to chew food and talk, and she easily chokes on nothing more than her own saliva. A doctor's error changed the quality of her life forever. But she chose not to sue the doctor. She believed that destroying his reputation would outweigh any temporary financial benefit she might receive. People often ask her whether she took the doctor to court, and she uses the opportunity to tell them how grateful she is for medical practitioners who are willing to put themselves at risk every day, knowing a simple error could cost them a reputation earned over a lifetime.

Every day Larry and Sue make choices about the reputations they're reflecting in the world through their words, attitudes, and influence. Both Larry and Sue make decisions that cut against the grain of today's "me-first" mind-set. Their stories remind us that our character becomes obvious in the tough moments of life when we're challenged. For those of us on the receiving end of health care, those challenges can come often.

Reputation is the calling card that allows us entrance into the hearts and lives of others. It's the foundation for respect, upon which people choose to listen to us or turn a deaf ear. We acquire our reputations through the accumulation of our words and actions. Without a positive reputation, we're limited in our ability to influence others and carry out our commission to make disciples in the world.

Ultimately, our reputation flows from our values. Proverbs 11:3 tells us that integrity guides us, but the unfaithful are destroyed by double-dealing. One biblical figure with a sterling reputation was Daniel. Daniel cared about his reputation. Even in the most difficult circumstances, he looked at long-term consequences, not merely for himself, but for God's greater glory. He forgave those who wronged him, served others, showed wisdom in his speech and actions, and ran from temptation. He was motivated by a desire to glorify God in everything he did—in spite of his circumstances. Daniel lived out the truth of 1 Corinthians 10:31: "So whatever you eat or drink or whatever you do, do it all for the glory of God."

Matthew 6:31–33 gives us the secret to a godly reputation: Don't worry about the things the world runs after. God will take care of us. Place His eternal values first. Work for the day we will hear the words, "Well done, good and faithful servant!" (Matthew 25:21).

Dear Father, may I place Your eternal values first in all that I do. Help me live in the truth that my reputation is secured in Your image but to be motivated by integrity and values that give me influence in the lives of others to draw them closer to You. Amen.

1. What values have influenced your reputation?

2. Jesus has already secured your reputation. How does this influence the way you conduct yourself on a day-to-day basis?

SECTION 3

Searching, Stretching, and Significance

My sin—O, the bliss of this glorious thought—
My sin not in part but the whole,
Is nailed to the cross, and I bear it no more,
Praise the Lord, praise the Lord, O my soul!

It is well with my soul,
It is well, it is well with my soul.

When I stand before God at the end of my life, I would hope that I would not have a single bit of talent left, and could say, "I used everything You gave me."

ERMA BOMBECK

When I was a child of ten or so, each day as I walked to school I prayed I'd have a "good" day. A "good" day for me was a day without teasing, snubbing comments, and condescending looks. I was a chubby kid, and although I was smart and got good grades, those things weren't enough. What I really wanted was to look a little bit more like the Barbie dolls that had suddenly taken over the world of little girls in the sixties.

As I grew older, my prayers for "good" days grew more adult. I prayed for my prodigal son to return home and to the God he'd professed to love as a child. I prayed for my daughter to be delivered safely home from the tsunami in Indonesia. I prayed for my mother to be delivered from the mental torment of Alzheimer's and my father-in-law to be released from the ravages of obsessive-compulsive disorder.

When we look at the chaos and suffering in our world, we can conclude that we're helpless to control our lives. According to DivorceRate.org, 50 percent of marriages end in divorce. More than 30 percent of American adults have abused alcohol or have suffered from alcoholism (http://on.msnbc.com/wcPeHV). One out of seven U.S. residents will be diagnosed with cancer, and one out

of five will die of heart disease (http://www.livescience.com/3780
-odds-dying.html). Only three out of ten teenagers who grew up
with a Christian background stay committed to church and their
faith after they graduate (David Kinnaman, *You Lost Me: Why Young
Christians Are Leaving Church . . . and Rethinking Faith* [Grand Rapids:
Baker, 2011]).

Most people spend their lives pursuing power, beauty, wealth,
and success. Few attain personal peace. Pop singing icon Madonna
has stated, "I have an iron will, and all of my will has always been
to conquer some horrible feeling of inadequacy . . . I push past one
spell of it and discover myself as a special human being, and then I
get to another stage and think I'm mediocre and uninteresting . . .
Again and again. My drive in life is from this horrible fear of being
mediocre. And that's always pushing me, pushing me. Because even
though I've become Somebody, I still have to prove I'm Somebody.
My struggle has never ended and it probably never will" (http://bit
.ly/8Pssav).

So where do we go to find purpose in life? Why are we here?

The Bible teaches us that this life is really about something
greater. Our time here is preparation for what's to come: heaven and
eternity with God. Our job—whether we're a parent, corporate ex-
ecutive, student, chef, best friend, auto mechanic, college professor,
or whoever we may be—is to get to heaven in the best shape possible
and to bring as many people with us as we can. As believers, we're
told that wisdom and purpose are defined by learning to "number
our days" (Psalm 90:12).

Are you struggling to become Somebody? Rest in knowing your
identity and significance are received and not earned. Learn to
number your days as you live out your God-given purpose.

DEPRESSION

When you pass through the waters, I will be with you; and when you pass through the rivers, they will not sweep over you. When you walk through the fire, you will not be burned; the flames will not set you ablaze.

ISAIAH 43:2

M y husband grew up in a household where his parents talked about depression about as often as they talked about the mating habits of Himalayan yaks. Dan's parents (and mine) were of the stoic post–World War II generation and were too busy to be depressed because they focused on making the world a better place and creating good lives for their families. Self-reflection wasn't part of their makeup.

So Dan was shocked when, during his college years, his mother revealed a family secret: his grandfather had committed suicide. Dan had known his Grandpa Beach had struggled financially and lost the family farm in Michigan during the height of the Great Depression. He'd known Grandma Beach had sold the homestead and moved to Houghton, New York, where she took in boarders and taught so her children could receive a Christian education. But no one had spoken about suicide or depression, perhaps because it was considered a weakness or sin or simply because no one had the words to shape it.

Decades later, when Dan's father, a retired missionary, came to live with us in the later years of his life, he could never find the words to talk about his own depression. Dan and I had noticed the signs of struggle in his father not long after we were married. Norman had just lost his beloved Marian after more than thirty years of marriage. Soon after her death, his love for solitude slipped into an alarming reclusiveness. His eating patterns changed, and he grew frighteningly thin. Eventually, friends called us and reported they rarely saw him at church. When they spoke to him, he struggled to communicate.

Dan and I were concerned. We drove to Missouri for a long weekend with his father and knew immediately something was gravely wrong. Within two weeks, we'd moved him into our home to explore medical answers.

We were convinced that, along with other medical problems, Norman was struggling with depression, yet we found it difficult to broach the topic with a godly missionary who seemed shamed by the subject. In spite of our fears, Dan and I knew we were responsible to seek the best care for Norman when he couldn't seek it himself. So Dan and I began our first foray into the mental health community. We didn't realize it would not be our last.

We sought recommendations and found the best doctors, psychiatrists, and Christian counselors. We were referred to a mental health facility, where Norman's condition was thoroughly assessed and the appropriate medications prescribed for his condition: Parkinson's disease, which often is accompanied by debilitating depression. Over the next year, we found the appropriate combination of medications that provided the most effective treatment for Norman's Parkinson's and depression.

The Christian community is sometimes skeptical about treating the brain as a physical organ with the same chemical and organic structure as other parts of the body. We sometimes create an unbiblical mind/body dichotomy that makes us reluctant to turn to drugs for answers to mental illnesses or depression. Unfortunately, this hesitation sometimes shames those who suffer from mental illnesses and turns into oversimplified solutions.

God, our Great Physician, is our healer in all things. The physiology of our body does not start at the shoulders, and we should always pursue the best possible treatments for illness, as we consider safety, side effects, medical recommendations, and the guidelines of Scripture for stewardship of our bodies. The use of anti-depressants or anti-psychotics can be a wise medical choice that promotes health and healing.

Our family is grateful to God that we found appropriate medications for Norman that allowed him to remain in our home for years after his diagnosis of Parkinson's disease. And we thank God for medical researchers and physicians who are working toward cures for mental illness and helping the families of those dealing with the challenges of these illnesses.

Father, the Psalms and other Scriptures show us people who were close to Your heart who struggled with depression. You are close to those who know heartache and are burdened. Lord, help me find the resources I need to battle the medical aspects of depression. And may I seek the truth of Your Word as the balm for my soul. Amen.

1. Has depression affected your family? How did you respond?

2. In what ways do you think Christians can create better means of support for those dealing with depression?

Because Your Mind Matters

Love the Lord your God with all your heart and with all your soul and with all your mind and with all your strength.

MARK 12:30

L ouann doesn't speak freely of her struggle with bipolar disorder. A successful author, editor, and now pastor of a church in the Midwest, she's found many people don't understand the challenges of mental illness. But she's discovered living with bipolar disorder has uniquely equipped her beyond her seminary training for ministry work.

Louann was born into a pastor's family that held high expectations. Although mental illness wasn't discussed much in her home, she discovered early in life that bipolar disorder ran in her family. Yet the household's unspoken assumption was that mental illness was somehow relegated to "other" people, and Louann never believed a diagnosis would affect her personally.

Ill health touched Louann's life in other ways. She was born with a painful medical condition called lymphedema. The condition blocks the lymphatic system in an arm or a leg and results in painful swelling. Those diagnosed with lymphedema require continual medical attention and often experience disfigurement. The pain and swelling from Louann's lymphedema were severe enough to limit her lifestyle and contribute to mood swings and depression. But she'd been taught that Christians shouldn't struggle with depression, and guilt plagued her.

In her twenties, Louann experienced a prolonged period of complications and severe pain related to her lymphedema. She was unable to sleep, and her anxiety increased. Before long, she slid into a state of severe anxiety, and her depression worsened. As her symptoms increased, her guilt grew, and she slid to an all-time low.

One day she experienced a new level of despair. In her pain, she cried out to God to take her to heaven. Her parents were terrified at the implications of her words and took her to a doctor to get a prescription to "take the edge off" her mental state. But Louann knew sedatives wouldn't be enough and made the decision to speak to her father. Her words left no room for negotiation: "Today is the day I'm going to get help." Her parents agreed and made an appointment with a psychiatrist who prescribed needed medications for depression.

Within a few weeks Louann was feeling better, but a friend helped her understand that, deep down, she was angry at God. She began journaling and talking to God about her feelings. Over the next few years her anger dissipated as she continued praying and journaling.

For months after starting treatment, Louann struggled. She went off and back on her medications a few times before her psychiatrist gave her a painful diagnosis: bipolar disorder. If she didn't take the appropriate medication for her illness consistently, the cycles of depression would continue, and she would never get better.

Louann shared the diagnosis with her parents, but they found it hard to believe. She was heartbroken, but she committed to taking her medication, even though it caused her to lose much of her hair.

In the years that followed, Louann experienced additional episodes with her bipolar disorder, and with each, she has learned more about how to handle her illness. Today she has not had a breakdown in five years. She has married, enrolled in seminary, and accepted a part-time pastoral position. She also continues to write and mentor other writers.

"Those of us with bipolar disorder can become trapped in a cycle of shame," she says. "We lose control over our lives because many times we can't control when episodes will occur. We feel like the disease and symptoms are our fault, even though that's not true. I hesitate to tell people I have bipolar disorder. It's easier to say it's depression. I can't control the perceptions of others, of course, but I can choose to embrace the truth for myself.

"I've learned that mental illness is not a reflection of our spirituality and relationship with God. I'm blessed because I had the opportunity to go through counseling along the way, and now I pass that wisdom along to those I pastor. My pain is being recycled.

"I have a greater heart to listen and to hear. I assure those who struggle with mental illness that medication and counseling are God's cup of cold water for those in need. I reassure them that God restores us to wholeness. We should never be ashamed. Although my illness is still with me, I've found incredible healing. And if I'm struck with another episode, God's equipped me with incredible coping skills to know what to do.

"Mental and physical weaknesses are gateways to God's ministry to us. He comes to us in our most broken places. He promises to fight with us and for us in *all* our needs—perhaps most of all in the battles for our mind."

Dear Father, nothing makes us feel more helpless than when illness strikes our minds. Thank You for medical resources that can address our needs. Give us wisdom to discern what is best for us. Open our eyes to the physicians, counselors, and resources that You make available to us. Surround us with Your presence, and help us to reject shame and to embrace Your perfect love and acceptance. Amen.

1. Have you or a loved one struggled with a mental illness? Have others refused to acknowledge the need for medical care for you or that person? How did it affect you?

2. How can our mental and emotional weaknesses be a gateway to God's ministry to us? Have you ever experienced this?

The Cries of the Afflicted

For he will deliver the needy who cry out, the afflicted who have no one to help.

PSALM 72:12

Twenty-four and a recent college graduate, Karen had taken a position as a full-time youth pastor and was ready to take on the world. She'd finally achieved her dream, and life should have been good. But she found herself sliding into a deep depression. As the weeks ticked by, her world transformed into a confusing maze of darkness and despair, and her family grew concerned.

Finally Karen agreed to admit herself to the mental health unit of her local hospital for a three-day stay. By the time she agreed, the real and the unreal had blurred into a world of delusions, and she was terrified. At the end of the three days, doctors came to her with a diagnosis: schizophrenia. They recommended she remain for further evaluation.

Karen refused to accept the diagnosis. After all, who would accept a youth pastor with a diagnosis of schizophrenia? Admitting her mental illness would mean the end of her career. She insisted on being released for the Christmas holidays against doctors' orders. Once she was home, she refused to take her medications and slid once again into a downward spiral. However, this time her family recognized her symptoms and committed her to a mental health unit against her protests.

Although she was angry at the time, today Karen admits that her family's move was an act of courage that could very well have saved her life. She was too unwell to discern what was best for herself, and she was unaware of how to battle the illness of schizophrenia. Like many who struggle with mental illness, she needed the advocacy of trusted loved ones.

Initially doctors saw limited improvement from the medications they prescribed for Karen, but a transfer to a mental health facility known for its successful treatment of schizophrenia patients proved to be an answer to prayer for Karen and her family. Several weeks later, she was released, greatly improved. Today she has returned to ministry and is employed as a youth pastor in the Midwest. She never lost her faith in God and always believed He would provide healing. Throughout her experience, Karen trusted her parents. They created a positive environment for her healing and restoration, and provided loving support and accountability. They helped her chart her progress and identify goals, allowing her to slowly take on responsibilities as she grew healthy again. Her mother and father reinforced positive change while reminding Karen of God's unconditional love for her. (Karen's mother now helps people in her community understand the challenges of schizophrenia and mental illness and leads advocacy and support groups.)

Karen's also grateful for the positive support of Christian friends and a strong church that helped when she was discouraged or needed accountability. And she's grateful for the skill of highly qualified psychiatrists and counselors who helped her regain control over the disease.

Karen admits that schizophrenia carries the stigma of shame.

She's careful about who she tells about her illness because it's difficult to predict how people will react. Non-Christians and even Christians have treated her disrespectfully because of her diagnosis. People often fear those with schizophrenia and believe they can't live normal, productive lives. However, Karen believes her life gives evidence to the contrary and is a testimony to a God who listens to the cries of His children in their darkest moments and offers hope and healing.

> *Dear God, help me trust those people You've placed in my life to give me wise counsel in the moments when life is confusing and circumstances seem out of control. Lead me to skilled doctors and mental health professionals. Let me show grace when people don't understand the confusion, fear, and uncertainty that I feel. Help me to trust You, even in the dark moments when I can't see what lies ahead. I know You are there, and Your love will never fail me. Amen.*

1. We often associate mental illness with shame. But in what ways is this a lie of Satan? Have you experienced shame? How did you deal with it?

2. Who has provided support for you in your illness, and what has that support looked like?

FINDING HOPE FOR POST-TRAUMATIC STRESS DISORDER

You will be secure, because there is hope; you will look about you and take your rest in safety.

JOB 11:18

Our family had gathered to celebrate Christmas in 2004. We were all present in our home in Michigan, with the exception of our daughter, Jessica, who was in Germany, training to be deployed for an overseas mission outreach. As our family sat in the living room the day after Christmas, watching TV and munching leftovers, a newscast interrupted the regularly scheduled programming: Indonesia had been devastated by the most massive tsunami in recorded history.

I watched in horror as people fled the wall of water rushing to sweep them away, as a wave of certainty swept into my own heart: "Jessica's going to that place, to those people. All of her training and preparation have been for this."

And I was right. Within weeks, Jessica's mission team was deployed to Nias Island—her organization's first team of relief workers to be sent in. No one on the team spoke the native language, and few were prepared for the overwhelming destruction. While working for another humanitarian agency, Jessica had trained in universal medical precautions and disaster intervention. She'd worked on mission teams in developing countries and had learned to live at a subsistence level. But nothing had prepared her for the devastation of Nias Island.

In just a few short months, she and her team had experienced more than a dozen earthquakes. She was taught to run to the top of a building during tremors and to "ride the building down" as it collapsed. Death surrounded her team—from the smells in the air to the sights in the streets.

Within days of her arrival, Jessica became so ill she was unable to walk. Her team—committed to delivering food and water to starving survivors—left her alone in a cracked and crumbling building while they went into the community each day. She lay weak, staring at the cracks in the walls around her, unable to flee to safety as aftershock after aftershock shook the building. During one particularly strong aftershock, the building next to theirs collapsed. The following day, the team moved to tents outdoors, where they were plagued by insects.

By the time Jessica returned to the States, her body, mind, and emotions had been ravaged. Panic attacks controlled her life. For days, she was unable to get out of bed. The sound of slamming doors or passing trucks triggered flashbacks. At times, she "zoned out" and drifted away in order to escape.

Dan and I had never heard of post-traumatic stress disorder (PTSD) and didn't know the symptoms. We had no idea what was wrong or how to help our daughter. Friends and family kindly suggested that she simply needed rest and prayer, and would soon "snap out of it." I prayed they were right, but Jess needed healing, and God graciously steered me in the direction of several Christians who were experts in post-traumatic stress disorder. One woman was a forensic psychologist with an international relief organization who traveled the world helping those who experienced "secondary" trauma assisting in the world's worst disasters. She and Jessica were able to connect through the Internet, and she helped ease Jessica's fears by assuring her that her symptoms were common.

My mother's heart wanted to hold my daughter close, but several months after Jessica's return, she announced she was taking a new job across the country. I was concerned about her decision, since she was under enormous stress. But I soon learned God had led her to a Christian community where the leadership was familiar with PTSD. She found a Christian psychiatrist and former missionary who specialized in post-traumatic stress disorder who understood her experiences, as well as the effects of trauma on the chemistry of the brain. Shortly after moving to Washington, Jessica was thriving once again. God had sent our daughter to a place where she could receive the right treatment.

God cares about our *every* need and provides resources we sometimes can't imagine. At times we may not take our fears and concerns to God because we think they're too big. At times we may be afraid He won't show up, and we'll be disappointed. But God's heart is moved by the things that keep us awake at night—the things that pull at our hearts during the day. And He's waiting for us to bring those concerns to Him, no matter what they may be, so He can respond. God is able to do exceedingly, abundantly above all we ask or think, and He delights in our requests. He's waiting to provide abundance beyond what we envision for ourselves. So trust and ask. He's waiting to hear from you.

Father, we know that You are the Healer, and all healing comes from You, whether through the science of medicine or the truth and understanding we receive through counseling. Thank You for the resources at our disposal today for health and healing. Lord, when our loved ones experience trauma, give us wisdom, courage, and gratitude to embrace treatments as healing gifts from You. Amen.

1. Post-traumatic stress disorder is associated with war, but it also affects those who have experienced physical and verbal abuse, traumatic medical procedures, violence, and life-threatening situations. What traumas have shaken your world? Where have you found hope and healing? Where are you still hurting?

2. How can the Christian community support those in need of counseling and treatment for PTSD?

Reaching Beyond Quadriplegia

I can do everything through him who gives me strength.

PHILIPPIANS 4:13

Growing up, Jill always expected that one day she'd be a wife and mother. A gifted child who grew to be a talented teen gymnast, she was performing a double backflip on a trampoline when she broke her neck. At the age of fourteen, she was diagnosed as a quadriplegic and told she'd live the remainder of her life without the use of her arms and legs. Her parents were told Jill would require twenty-four-hour care, and it was unlikely she'd ever regain movement below her neck.

Over the next years, Jill focused on learning how to do things differently and developed the use of the muscles in her shoulders and upper arms. Unlike many people who are injured traumatically, Jill struggled only briefly with depression and instead focused on what she *could* do. Jill didn't try to muster up an optimistic attitude. She believes God guarded her heart from dark nights of despair and discouragement about what life would be like in a wheelchair.

When Jill was nineteen, she was asked to counsel teens who'd been injured at the Columbine High School shooting. At the event she met Brooks Gibbs, a handsome, energetic youth speaker. The two fell in love and married. Jill was determined to be the best wife and mother she could be. When the time came to think about childrearing, Jill and Brooks discussed how they could creatively approach the complications of Jill's quadriplegia. They were convinced God would help them figure out how to be the best possible parents, in spite of her limitations.

For instance, Jill can't hold a child and wheel her chair at the same time. Maneuvering babies in and out of car seats is also difficult, since she lacks fine motor skills. Handicapped bathroom stalls can be challenging, since they're often too small to use with a wheelchair, an adult, and a child. And if all the handicapped spots are taken in a parking lot, Jill is often forced to drive around until a spot becomes available.

Parenting presents daily frustrations for Jill, yet she doesn't allow herself to become negative. (She admits she has an occasional good cry, and then lets things go.) She's honest about the reality that she can't do things as easily as other people and doesn't let herself get lost in "what ifs." She allows herself more time to accomplish tasks and accepts that God has assigned her the job of fulfilling her beloved role of wife and mother from a wheelchair.

Certain parenting realities do sadden Jill. For instance, when her oldest son wanted to ride on the New York subway, Jill and Brooks explained that they couldn't get Mom's chair down the stairs. Jill would love to take her sons into the yard and throw a ball with them, and she wishes she'd had the opportunity to hold her boys more frequently when they were babies. But she's also grateful that in spite of her injury, she does have the capability to hold her sons, travel, and enjoy activities with her family.

Jill focuses on walking through each day with the Lord and trusting that He's in control. Her advice for other women who mother with handicaps? "God gave *you* to your child. He loves your child even more than you do. He chose you to be your child's mother, and your children aren't getting the short end of the stick. Parenting may be difficult, but you're the right parent for your son or daughter.

"Brooks and I have noticed a different level of compassion in our boys that they've learned from living with someone with a disability. They're aware of needs because they live with my limitations on a daily basis. They might not get to do everything other children do, but they're developing character.

"Take your parenting one day at a time. Present your trials and frustrations to the Lord, and ask Him for comfort. God knows what I'd like to do with my boys each day, and He's always faithful to give us the things we need most, whether or not they look like the things I'd always choose first."

Dear Father, today I'm bringing You my trials and frustrations. You know each and every detail. Please comfort me as only You can, and provide exactly what I need for today. Help me give my unfulfilled expectations to You, trusting You're working out a plan for me. Amen.

1. How do you feel about Jill's approach of having an occasional cry and then moving on?

2. What does it mean for you to take your trials and frustrations to the Lord to ask Him for comfort?

SMALL THINGS

For who has despised the day of small things?
ZECHARIAH 4:10 (NKJV)

It was Sunday evening, and my husband Dan and I had arrived at church for the evening service: thirty minutes of singing in the auditorium before our congregation split into groups for Sunday school classes. It was one of our favorite times of the week.

We entered the auditorium at the rear and stopped as one of our pastors greeted us.

"We're doing something a little different tonight. We'll be circling up in small groups for singing and discussion instead of heading to our usual classes."

I scanned the room and the chairs that had been drawn into circles and felt panic rising in my throat. Not a row in the place. I turned and glanced at Dan to see if the significance had dawned on him. Nope—no light in the swamp. He had no idea a booby trap had been set for the likes of us. He smiled innocently and headed for the closest circle, where several of our friends had gathered.

"And what do you think our plan should be?" I whispered as I followed beside him.

Dan glanced at me, a blank expression on his face. "Our plan?"

"Yes. Our plan for not falling down. I really don't want to be added entertainment for the church tonight."

"Not falling down? What are you talking . . ." Then, slowly, a look of horror dawned. "We're doomed, aren't we?"

Dan and I both have a neurological condition that has damaged the nerves in our feet and legs, and those nerves now have trouble communicating with our brains. The result? Like Weeble-Wobble toys, we teeter and totter, but sometimes we *do* fall down, especially when we don't have something to hang on to.

When we're in public, we position ourselves strategically near walls and tables. Put us in the middle of a room, and we sway and jerk, creating the illusion that all we really want to do is crank up a little Chubby Checker so we can twist and shout. When we're in church, we hold on for dear life to the chairs in front of us. That evening we got creative. People in our circle probably thought we were the cuddliest love bugs ever. But out of sheer self-preservation, we laced our bodies together and fought to stay upright as we swayed from side to side throughout the singing like weeping willows in the wind.

A brain lesion and neuropathy have made me grateful for small things: handrails, chair backs, sturdy walls, my husband's hand, and a sense of humor. My neurological condition is progressive, which increases my gratitude today for the things I may not have tomorrow.

May I never lose my gratitude for the small things in life, and may I never cease to be grateful to God, who blesses me in all things, both small and great.

Father, may I never lose a heart of gratitude and eyes to see the thousand ways You bless me. Even in moments of suffering, let me notice the things You're doing to care for me—to protect me and go before me and provide for me. Help me remember that Your love surrounds me in every moment. Amen.

1. How do you remain grateful for the small things? What do you appreciate today that you may not have tomorrow?

2. How does gratitude influence other areas of life?

A Sermon in Shoes

Pursue righteousness, godliness, faith, love,
endurance and gentleness.

1 Timothy 6:11

Open my closet, and my shoes will tell you a story.

Pumps, sling backs, sandals, and spike heels are neatly nested in a vertical storage bag, snugly stacked in boxes, and lined in toe-touching rows along the floor. Dozens of pairs in black, brown, navy, red, camel, and other hues and styles to match the need of the occasion. The silver spike heels with satin bows at the heels are my favorite—worn for a toe-pinching two hours during an awards ceremony, and then unceremoniously kicked beneath the table and later slung by their straps over my patient husband's arm.

One distinctive pair of shoes sits at the front of the closet—black and utilitarian, the shoes I've worn day after day for the past two years. The toe box of the left shoe is scraped and scuffed from a lazy leg that drags when I'm tired. They are lightweight and shock absorbing, and don't graze my toes or hug the tops of my feet, setting off the cascade of electrical shocks that torture my feet and legs after I go to bed at night. I am already dreading the day when I'll be forced to replace them and begin my angst-ridden search for a new pair.

Because of my neuropathy, I haven't worn any of the dozens of pairs of "cute" shoes in my closet for years. Yet each time I pack them up to give them away, they somehow make their way back into my closet.

Why, you might ask?

A voice inside my head tells me that someday (hopefully before pointy toes go out of style again), my feet will once again be well enough to tolerate wearing pretty shoes. The voice tells me to hold on to hope—that this insidious disease and its pain can be healed— that *I* can and will be healed. And so my shoes remain in my closet, collecting dust.

As believers in Jesus Christ, we're told to "hold on" while we're here on earth. First Timothy 6:12 encourages us to "fight the good fight of the faith. Take hold of the eternal life to which you were called when you made your good confession in the presence of many witnesses." But how are we able to do this?

In spite of what I experience, I can live with an eternal perspective. Jesus has secured my healing. I'm promised a glorified, pain-free body like His own body. God may choose to heal me here on earth, but His plan may also be served by my suffering, like His Son. So in spite of my circumstances, I continue to hope. In spite of my circumstances, I hold on.

This week as I hope and hold on, I'm also letting go. A mission in our community provides business clothing to abused women re-entering the work force. Tonight my closet will be cleaner and my heart lighter. Several dozen pairs of cute shoes will find a new purpose and new homes.

But the spike-heeled silver shoes will stay. Sometimes "hope" wears satin bows at the heels.

Dear Father, thank You that I don't have to be afraid. While circumstances change, You do not change. Because I have You, I lack nothing. You alone are sufficient for all my needs. Amen.

1. What does it mean for you to "fight the good fight" in the moments when life is painful, unfair, and nonsensical?

2. Have you held on to tangible symbols of hope? In what ways have they helped you sustain a visible reminder of God's promises?

Eyes for the Mission

Be watchful, and strengthen the things which remain . . .
REVELATION 3:2 (KJV)

I f actions speak louder than words, Dennis Booker's life shouted praise to God. No matter where he was or who he was with, he shared his love for Jesus in ways people could see and feel. The world was his mission field, and he refused to let people, circumstances, or life's challenges stand in the way of a lived-out faith.

As a husband, Dennis adored his precious Sue, the center of his life and the sweetheart he'd fallen in love with in high school. They supported each other through more than thirty-five years of marriage, until the day Sue's life was taken by a drunk driver.

As a father, Dennis was devoted to his seven children, taking them camping and fishing, and teaching them to "do right" in spite of the cost. In his community, he was the "neighborhood dad" who invested in the lives of troubled kids—many who later thanked him for walking beside them during the toughest times of their lives. As the first black police detective in Grand Rapids, Michigan, Dennis earned a reputation for commitment and integrity among fellow officers. He retired as sergeant after twenty-five years of service, winning Grand Rapids Community College's prestigious Walter Coe Public Service Award for "exceptional contributions shaping the history and quality of life of greater Grand Rapids."

Dennis Booker wasn't handed an easy life; he was one of many black Americans who faced the challenges of a changing nation. He and Sue raised their family during the racial unrest of the civil rights movement. Dennis's son Mike remembers one instance when his father refused to respond to a racial slur on the job. Mike had accompanied his father, at the time a security guard at a downtown building, to work. During the course of a conversation, a white co-worker sneered at Dennis and referred to him as "boy."

Mike was outraged to see someone disrespect his father, but his dad later told him, "Son, don't let what he said bother you. It's not that man talking—those words come from the devil. Racial attacks are spiritual warfare."

"Dad taught me to use everything for God," Mike states. "Life isn't about us."

Dennis found his final mission field when his health failed after the death of his wife, and he moved into the Grand Rapids Home for Veterans. Although the transition would mean leaving the home he loved, he used the experience to glorify God with his positive attitude as he adjusted to roommates and learned to live in community. Dennis was excited about new opportunities to tell others about the God he loved. Residents remember Brother Booker as the smiling man who rode the halls in his electric cart inviting people to church and Bible studies. He encouraged residents and staff and was known as a prayer warrior.

Dennis Booker embodied a missional mind-set. No matter his circumstances, he couldn't be stopped from talking about the God he loved. He invested his final years at the Home for Veterans the same way he'd invested his time with his family, in his career, and in the earlier years of his life—creating opportunities to tell others about the Savior he loved.

Father, give me a vision for others, no matter where I am or where I may be called to serve in life. May I never lose a heart for You that compels me to serve others. Amen.

1. How can our attitude influence our choices and even our sense of purpose during the difficult transitions in life?

2. How are you preparing for transitions that will mean greater dependency in upcoming years?

REDIRECTION

The Lord will fight for you; you need only to be still.

EXODUS 14:14

⸎

Jeff invested thirty-five years in ministry as a pastor, serving in three Midwestern churches where he and his family were loved, and his churches grew and thrived. Over the years, he ministered to thousands of individuals and families, and young pastors often came to him for counsel and direction.

One Sunday morning as Jeff was preaching, searing pain shot down his arm and spread to his chest. He struggled for breath, but it seemed as if the weight of the building had collapsed on his body. He was rushed to a nearby hospital, where doctors diagnosed him with a medical condition that had invaded his lungs, spleen, liver, and kidneys, and was damaging his heart. Over the following months, Jeff's condition deteriorated, and he was put on a heart transplant list.

As he lay in a specialized cardiac care unit, Jeff pondered his future. It was unlikely he'd ever have the strength to pastor again. Doctors advised him to talk to his wife about the limitations of his condition and to consider early retirement. Suddenly, everything

Jeff had known was in question—his identity, future, security, his very life. At the moment when he wanted most to fight, he was being asked to be still and trust God. As a pastor whose life had been leading and directing others, Jeff suddenly felt uncertain about trusting God when he felt helpless to do anything.

After years of captivity in Egypt, the children of Israel fled, only to discover that the Red Sea lay between them and freedom. They saw no way to get through or around this massive body of water and were overwhelmed by feelings of defeat, questioning God's plan: Why did you bring us here to die?

God reminded His children through Moses, first of all, that their faith would be evidenced by their actions (Exodus 14:13–18). First, they were told to stand firm and wait for God's deliverance. Then they were told to move and pass through the divided sea. Hebrews 11:1 tells us that faith consists of both our hope and the unseen. But faith is not passive. It moves us forward, and the children of Israel were asked to press toward the object of their hope in order to achieve God's promise.

Because God wants us to trust Him, He asks all of us to step out in faith—sometimes at the most painful moments of our lives. For Jeff, steps of faith included considering early retirement and finding a way to redirect his talents. And although the decision was painful, he withdrew from full-time leadership in his church. He became involved with a mentoring ministry for young pastors, and today he's multiplying his pastoral ministry as he invests in the lives of future church leaders.

No matter our circumstances, Our Deliverer always shows up. We can depend on God—who held back the waters of the Red Sea so the children of Israel could walk safely through—to fight for us and deliver us in our battles. But waiting for deliverance isn't passive. God requires that we do our part, to step out in faith and move forward.

Active faith believes God's promises. Active faith leans upon God's character. Active faith claims God's promised future. Active faith is grateful in all circumstances. Active faith rests in God's goodness.

Whatever battle you're facing, you can be comforted in knowing your Father God fights on your behalf and goes before you.

Lord, You know it's difficult for me to be still when I want to control my circumstances. But You go before me and fight on my behalf, working in ways I cannot see. May I choose an active faith that rests in your character and proclaims your goodness in all things. Help me to tune out the babble of my own voice and listen for You to speak to me. Amen.

1. When have you been asked to step between parted waters and exercise your faith? What was the outcome?

2. What hinders you from moving forward in faith? Are you facing any of those circumstances at this moment? If so, how is God speaking to you right now?

The Power of Prayer

For this reason, since the day we heard about you, we have not stopped praying
for you and asking God to fill you with the knowledge of his will through all
spiritual wisdom and understanding.

Colossians 1:9

I was fourteen the day Miss Edith invited me to her home and insisted I pick out a favorite piece of furniture. My favorite Sunday
school teacher from the days she let me wiggle flannelgraph camels
across a watercolor fabric desert, Miss Edith reminded me of Angela
Lansbury: her ash-brown hair upswept in a neat chignon, her fin-
gernails neatly manicured, and her full-figured body decked out in
close-fitting, stylish suits.

Among the various fascinations that set Miss Edith apart were
her independent singleness and the distinction of being the voice
of our local telephone company recordings. Whenever I heard the
familiar timbre of her voice telling me a number I'd dialed had been
disconnected, a strange thrill washed over me, as though I knew a
movie star personally. Her home boasted colorful Princess phones
in pastel colors in every room, which placed her in a category, in my
book, somewhere next to rock star.

Miss Edith lived in a tidy yellow house on Broadway Boulevard, where she superintended the care of her mother, who lived in a nursing home across the street. I'd known Miss Edith since I was born because she'd taught at our church for about as many years as it had taken the children of Israel to cross the desert.

Like most of the kids at my church, I loved Miss Edith. She knew how to make the Bible come alive, and by the time we were teenagers, we couldn't wait to get into her classes. She made mean homemade pastries and took her students to the beach and art shows and on trips to Bible colleges and the big city, like Chicago. Mostly, she loved us well and showed us that older adults could be cool and wise and quirky and fun and godly all at the same time.

Miss Edith's true secret power lay in her prayer life. On that day when I was fourteen and she invited me to pick out a piece of furniture that would someday be mine, I chose her drop-down desk, stacked high with prayer notebooks. Later I'd learn her desk was her favorite spot to pray for "her kids" and journal prayer requests into a notebook—even after we'd graduated, gone to college, married, and had children.

Miss Edith was perhaps the most powerful and consistent spiritual force in the lives of generations of young people who passed through my church. She, like countless other prayer warriors across the nation, fought unseen battles of spiritual warfare on behalf of others who never knew the power she wielded on their behalf. While we may never know the measure of her influence here on earth, we will see the results of her prayers in heaven. Her prayers influenced the lives of her spiritual "children" here on earth and into eternity.

Like Miss Edith, we may never see the results of our prayers here on earth. Yet may we all be committed to influencing lives—not only in this generation, but the generations that follow—through commitment to persistent prayer.

Dear Father, give me a vision for the hearts and lives of others. Give me diligence and discernment as I learn to be a prayer warrior for Your kingdom. Teach me to pray, Lord, and give me Your own heart. Amen.

1. How have the generations of your family been influenced by the prayers of others?

2. How is God using you to influence the world for His kingdom through the power of your prayers?

Family, Forgiveness, and Freedom

For me, be it Christ, be it Christ hence to live:
If Jordan above me shall roll,
No pang shall be mine, for in death as in life,
Thou wilt whisper Thy peace to my soul.

It is well with my soul,
It is well, it is well with my soul.

Forgiveness is the final form of love.

REINHOLD NIEBUHR

I love caller ID. This useful tool makes it possible for me to lob the phone to Dan in defensive maneuvers, dodge telemarketers, or finish browning the ground beef before calling a friend back. It also gives me the freedom to just say no and not pick up. And it allows me time to roll my eyes toward the ceiling and shoot a prayer heavenward before answering a call from Charlene.

Charlene is a sweet friend who's spent the last thirty years rehearsing the three hundred and eighty-six ways her in-laws have made her life miserable. She finds them insensitive and demanding. They're spending her inheritance on "frivolities" like surgery to replace pacemaker batteries and dental work. They ask to be driven to medical appointments. (Charlene's in-laws are in their eighties and live in Los Angeles.) They don't dress the way she would dress, cook the way she would cook, read what she would read, or breathe the way she would breathe. I have yet to have a conversation with Charlene in which she has said something positive about her in-laws that wasn't sarcastic.

Yet Charlene believes her in-laws are the problem. She fails to see that she casts the glare of ingratitude and unforgiveness like high beam headlights. Charlene sees everything through the spirit she projects, and her negative attitude can make people reluctant to approach her.

I should know. For many years, I wrapped myself in ingratitude and unforgiveness like my favorite winter coat. They were my protection and insulation against my deficits, faults, and sins. During the time I was blind to my negativity, others steered around me to escape the poison of my attitude.

Forgiveness and gratitude shape our relationships. Our ability to forgive flows from our gratitude for the abundant forgiveness we've received. Gratitude gives us the grace to resolve emotional conflict and signals a heart tethered to God. A spirit of gratitude must be fed by our awareness of what we've been given and who we are. When we don't allow gratitude and forgiveness to guide us through hurt, loss, and conflict, we become trapped in a self-centered, victim mentality.

Our ingratitude in hurtful circumstances and lack of forgiveness for frustrating people indicates, at the core, dissatisfaction with God; we're depending upon others to meet needs that are ultimately met in God alone. Even our "prickly" relationships are a gift from God because they're an opportunity to draw closer to Him as we learn to express His grace toward others.

We are not entitled to the self-righteous attitudes we so often justify. As sons and daughters of the Most High, we are prisoners of grace, compelled by gratitude to forgive.

For me, answering that call has meant releasing the wounds of my childhood. It's meant forgiving the serial rapist who attacked me when I was a teenager. It's meant forgiving the man who molested my child. And it's even meant dropping my self-righteous attitude, refusing to roll my eyes when Charlene calls, and listening with my heart.

Perhaps nowhere do we have greater opportunity to exercise the powers of gratitude and forgiveness than among our family members. May we be willing to crucify self-righteousness, pride, and anger as love compels us to serve.

A Victim Mentality

It is for freedom that Christ has set us free. Stand firm, then, and do not let yourselves be burdened again by a yoke of slavery.

GALATIANS 5:1

I hesitate as my fingers hover over the numbers on my phone. How many times have I made this call? How many times have my friends heard me repeat my excuses? I envision their sighs, their shrugs, their eye rolls. I imagine the frustrated reactions that run through their minds.

"Of *course* she's not coming. *Again.* Another excuse. *Again.* Why do we even bother to ask her?"

I glance at the clock and calculate the time. I could pull it off if I just put my mind to it. I'd only have to fake it for an hour or two. I've been doing it for years. Hiding the pain. Skimming along on the surface of conversation. Interjecting occasional comments. Straining to stay engaged.

Over the years, I'd given in to saying no to opportunities and invitations, rather than having to explain over and over what it's like to live inside a body I can't count on. And all the while, I'd carefully tended and fed my victim mentality.

Not that I would have recognized my self-centered mind-set for the first five years or so after I became ill. I couldn't admit what I couldn't see. Apart from the grace of God, I could have carried on for the rest of my life, blind to my twisted thinking. Thank God for some straight-talking people who loved me enough to sit me down for a good talking-to and a church that held up the mirror of God's Word to my heart. Once I recognized I'd allowed a victim mind-set to control my outlook on life, I knew I had to destroy it.

What did that victim mind-set look like? Victims look for validation and approval. I'd sought those things in "spiritual" places: church involvement, caregiving, teaching, and parenting. Victims are afraid to risk failure and rejection. I always played to my strengths, making sure I volunteered for things I was good at. But perhaps my greatest success as a victim was my skill at blaming other people. I was a pro. Just ask my kids or my husband.

So what did it take to break my victim mentality? The first step was seeing my heart as God saw it. My brokenness was the starting place for the Holy Spirit to begin the work of transformation. I learned to evaluate my false thinking according to God's standard of truth—the Bible. Scripture taught me that I had to take responsibility for my life and stop blaming God and others for family problems, bumpy friendships, job hassles, and the pain in my life. I had to learn to see from a new perspective, a biblical perspective.

If Scripture was trustworthy, I had to be willing to bring everything in my life into alignment with the Word of God. And I had to trust the Bible for what it said about *me*. I couldn't hang my identity on something as unpredictable as other people's opinions or my own works. God accepted me, so I was pretty amazing. I no longer had anything to prove.

Over the years, I've learned that gratitude moves our focus away from ourselves and onto others, and that forgiveness frees us from the chains of the past so we can move forward to serve. We are set free to serve, not to prove ourselves or earn approval, but to demonstrate gratitude for what we've been given.

What about you? Have you been set free from self-centeredness and a victim mentality? Are you free to love and serve out of a heart of gratitude?

> *Dear Father, I recognize that I try to put myself at the center of everything. May Your Spirit expose the lies in my thinking, the deceptions that keep me blind to my victim mentality. May Your Word convict me of truth, and may I be willing to conform my thinking to Your Word as I grow in gratitude and grace. Amen.*

1. What aspects of a victim mentality have you struggled with? Do you still struggle with?

2. How do you use Scripture to confront lies in your thinking?

THE FRACTURED FAMILY

From everlasting to everlasting the Lord's love is with those who fear him,
and his righteousness with their children's children.

PSALM 103:17

Living in a crisis mode began for the Anderson family the day Linda learned she was pregnant with triplets. Before the end of her second trimester, her gynecologist ordered twenty-four-hour bed rest. To help care for their six-year-old son and four-year-old daughter, the family hired a nanny, and Tom did his best to take extra hours away from his real estate business so he could spend time with Linda and the kids.

In Linda's third trimester, despite the best efforts of doctors, one of the triplets died. In her thirty-fifth week, she went into labor, giving birth to twin daughters who were just three pounds apiece and critically ill. Chloe lived just six days; Charity was born with cerebral palsy. Doctors predicted she would be deaf, blind, and mentally impaired. They encouraged Tom and Linda to place their daughter in an institutional setting where she could receive twenty-four-hour care.

The Andersons chose to keep Charity at home. Over time, she

astounded doctors by defying all medical predictions. Not only could she see and hear, but she was incredibly bright and socially interactive. However, the challenges of her cerebral palsy required constant medical intervention. The Andersons lived three hours from the children's hospital where Charity received her medical care, and over the ensuing years, the family often lived in separate worlds—Linda and Charity at the hospital and Tom and the two older children at home. Charity underwent more than fifty operations and suffered numerous strokes. The family bounced from crisis to crisis, trying to balance the needs of the entire family.

When a child is diagnosed with special needs or a life-threatening illness, or dies, the divorce rate is higher than average (http://www.disaboom.com/children-with-disabilities/for-better-or-worse-and-kids-with-disabilities). Stress levels skyrocket, and the family fragments. Siblings may isolate or act out. Spouses often grieve differently and may become withdrawn or angry. Family members who aren't ill often struggle with guilt, isolation, blame, and shame. The child who is ill often battles anger, resentment, guilt, and fear. Even families who have a deep faith in God need to develop strategies that will help them deal with complex emotions and long-term situations. Consider the following tips.

Don't carry the burden alone. Find friends, advocates, counselors, and social workers who will support your family.

Be patient with each other. You're all hurting, and you'll hurt in different ways.

Seek out counseling and/or support groups. Family members need to talk freely and share their concerns with others who have experienced similar struggles. Consider family counseling or individual counseling, depending on your particular needs. Support groups in your area can include Gilda's Clubs, the Parent/Professional Advocacy League (PAL), or groups specific to your child's illness.

Be aware of pressure points. What things stress you most? What about the kids? Are you addressing fear, anger, and other issues in healthy ways?

Whether married, divorced, widowed, or single, we all experience the fracturing of family that comes from the stress of illness. May we wisely face the burdens that can tear us from those we love.

Dear Father, I bring my needs and the needs of my family to you. The challenges of illness have brought resentment and isolation, guilt and shame into our family. May I be willing to look into my heart and take responsibility for any hurt I may have caused. Give me grace to forgive and wisdom to understand when others pull away or speak in anger. May we learn to love one another more as You have loved us. Amen.

1. Has the long-term pressure of separation or hospitalization affected your family? How did you handle the pain, the isolation, and the confusion?

2. Has your family experienced "fracturing"? How have you handled it? Do you believe God still desires you to take steps toward reconciliation and healing?

The Tough Side of Forgiveness

. . . forgiving each other, just as in Christ God forgave you.

EPHESIANS 4:32

B efore I became ill in 1999, I hadn't spent much time in hospitals, except for the Cesarean section births of my children,
where I was given lots of drugs, and a tonsillectomy when I was five,
where I was given lots of Popsicles. So for a long time, I thought all
doctors were knights on white horses who spoke kind words, kept
you happy, and smiled sweetly as they peered over the tops of their
glasses.

Until I was admitted to a hospital north of Detroit and learned
the Real Truth. Doctors, like the rest of us, have their bad days. The
day I was admitted with my brain lesion, I was assigned to the care
of a doctor who was having a bad day.

From my perspective, the "bad" part of the day belonged to me.
I'd arrived at the emergency room too sick to walk. My doc had
ordered tests and assigned me a room, and I'd settled in while supportive family arrived to wait for test results with me and offer
encouragement.

The doctor returned in the afternoon with test results. I'd

experienced a brain bleed. The MRI had revealed a large spot near my brain stem. He recommended a craniotomy—a procedure that would remove my skull so a surgeon could explore my medical condition more fully.

I was sick, but not too sick to know I didn't want brain surgery in a small-town hospital. But I didn't have to say a word. Immediately my family asked that I be transferred to Detroit Medical Center.

The doctor raised his eyebrows. So his hospital wasn't good enough?

My family stood their ground and requested an ambulance transfer.

He refused and shamed my husband with a few rude and condescending comments.

From my perspective, things seemed pretty clear. My brain was bleeding. I couldn't walk. I was seeing two of everything. If I was sick enough for brain surgery, I was sick enough for an ambulance. But a doctor's ego separated me from access to the care I needed.

The ride to the hospital was a nightmare I'll never forget. I was angry at that doctor for a very long time. I have to admit I felt a flush of self-righteous vindication when I heard he faced his own diagnosis a year later and chose to leave not only his hospital but the state to seek medical treatment.

But the truth of the matter is that, no matter how I *felt* about my mistreatment, I was responsible for forgiving the doctor. Forgiveness isn't a feeling. It's not forgetting. It's not pretending the doctor's actions didn't hurt. It's not signing back on as his patient. It's not adding him to my Christmas list or even trusting him. Forgiveness is a decision to obey God.

Forgiveness means I give up what the world defines as "my rights": my right to seek payback, my right to malign someone's reputation (even if what I'm saying is true), my right to hurt people in retaliation. Forgiveness means I let God even the score. I trust Him for justice and vindication.

Forgiveness requires me to give up my desire to control the person who hurt me and relinquish him or her to God. Then I allow the decision to forgive to shape my attitude, and my attitude affects my choices, my thinking, and my tongue. Ultimately forgiveness affects my relationship with God. "Forgive us our debts, as we also have forgiven our debtors," Jesus taught us to pray (Matthew 6:12). He goes on to state that our level of forgiveness for others influences whether or not God forgives us: "For if you forgive men when they sin against you, your heavenly Father will also forgive you. But if you do not forgive men their sins, your Father will not forgive your sins" (vv. 14–15). Forgiveness is where the rubber meets the road in our faith walk.

How do I know when I've forgiven? When God's love flows through me to the individual who's wronged me. Does this take place in an instant? No. For most of us, forgiveness is a process and often a daily decision to grant the grace we've so freely received. For me, that's meant praying for the doctor who refused me the dignity of an ambulance ride. It's meant learning to love him as I love myself, which means desiring and even working toward his best interests.

As a believer, I'm called to pass on what I've been given. The call to forgiveness isn't easy, but it's only as we learn to forgive that we gain the heart of Jesus.

Dear Father, You have forgiven me more than I could ever begin to understand. As I see glimpses of that forgiveness, help me to extend it freely to those around me, in spite of what may seem to be the cost. Help me to see the true value of forgiving others and extending Your grace. Thank You for Your gift of redemption that makes forgiveness possible. Amen.

1. Who do you have difficulty forgiving? Why? In what ways do you still fight to control people and situations?

2. What does it mean for you to grant grace to those who need forgiveness?

LAUGHTER

A cheerful heart is good medicine, but a crushed
spirit dries up the bones.

PROVERBS 17:22

Last year I received a call that my dear friend Wanda had been admitted to a hospital in California with serious respiratory problems. I quickly scheduled a flight and was at her side the following afternoon. I was shocked to see how ill she was. Her oxygen saturation, which should have been in the mid to high nineties, had dropped into the eighties, and doctors had placed her on oxygen. Her skin was a steely gray, and her eyes were sunken and ringed by dark circles.

Over the next few days, she was given numerous tests, and we waited in what is often referred to as the limbo of "hospital time." I was road weary from a rigorous speaking and travel schedule, and Wanda was drained from lack of sleep and the strain of months of ill health. As a combo, we were more than a few sandwiches short of a picnic and found the simplest things hilarious. On more than one occasion, nurses poked their heads into the room to discover the reason why two grown women were laughing uproariously.

On one particularly boring afternoon, I improvised a stand-up routine with a plastic emesis basin for a microphone, and, for reasons neither of us can remember, I placed Wanda's bra rakishly on my head.

Why, you might ask?

Because Wanda needed a gut-wrenching, belly-busting laugh that would lift her spirits and carry oxygen to nooks and crannies of her lungs that hadn't seen the stuff in far too long. And it worked. Today, all we have to do is begin the story of that experience, and we dissolve into laughter.

Proverbs tells us a cheerful heart is good medicine. But a "cheerful heart" goes beyond an occasional laugh. The term refers to an attitude and a lifestyle: a smile, a positive outlook, a willingness to look at the best in someone or offer a word of encouragement. Laughter and a joyful spirit are often contagious and can help others heal. Proverbs 17:22 explains why: "A cheerful heart is good medicine, but a crushed spirit dries up the bones."

A cheerful heart is rooted in quiet confidence and gratitude; it recognizes the greatness of God and takes time to praise: "Shout for joy to the Lord, all the earth. Worship the Lord with gladness; come before him with joyful songs" (Psalm 100:1–2). A cheerful heart also seeks intimacy with God through the power of the Holy Spirit and prayer: "Do not be anxious about anything, but in everything, by prayer and petition, with thanksgiving, present your requests to God. And the peace of God, which transcends all understanding, will guard your hearts and your minds in Christ Jesus" (Philippians 4:6–7). A cheerful heart also confidently presses toward God's purpose: "Let us run with perseverance the race marked out for us" (Hebrews 12:1). Because we know our purpose, we can operate confidently in the knowledge of who we are and what we are called to do.

You'll probably never feel moved to place underwear on your head to encourage a friend in Christ, but we should all listen for the voice of God calling us to laugh with friends, lift their spirits, and yes, to indulge in moments of hilarity.

Dear Father, may my life be one that causes others to smile, to laugh, and to fall more in love with You. May I bring Your infectious joy and healing to all I meet. Amen.

1. How does quiet confidence empower us to laugh and bring joy to others?

2. What place has laughter had in your walk of faith?

BROKEN CHAINS

From everlasting to everlasting the Lord's love is with those who fear him,
and his righteousness with their children's children.

PSALM 103:17

W hen Chuck Colson was sentenced to prison in 1973, approximately 229,000 inmates were housed in the American penal system. Today over 2.5 million prisoners are incarcerated, more than the combined populations of Vermont and West Virginia. The statistics are troubling, and the question government, communities, and churches should be asking is how our society can more effectively influence people to choose to live moral lives.

As a speaker with Daughters of Destiny prison ministry, I bring a message of hope and change to broken, hurting women across the nation. Each year I speak to thousands of inmates whose relationships with family members have been crushed or destroyed. The women I meet often plead with me to pray for their children, believing they have created irreparable legacies of pain and devastation.

But Jesus can heal all wounds. One of the prayer warriors who stands behind me in my ministry is my dear friend Ellen. She was once a felon, sought by the FBI and incarcerated for crimes against her children, among other things. For years, she and her husband defied the law, and their children paid a price. In the 1970s, Ellen and her husband were arrested, given long prison sentences, and taken from their children. Their hearts were hard, and they seemed beyond redemption and hope until visiting ministry teams in two separate prisons presented the good news of Jesus Christ. Through the grace of God, both Ellen and her husband came into a personal relationship with Jesus Christ.

The years that followed weren't easy, but Ellen and her husband had found a real faith. They grew in their commitment to God. They became involved in church and found mentors. They sought forgiveness and reconciled with their children. Fast-forward several decades to today, and by the grace of God, you'll find Ellen's family whole and healthy—sons, daughters, nieces, nephews, grandchildren, aunts, and uncles. They are productive members of society, supporting and loving one another.

Ellen and her husband didn't decide to live moral lives. They chose to accept a Savior whose power changed their hearts. Jesus Christ broke the chains of their past and created a new legacy for their family.

Are you discouraged, believing the choices or actions of your past have created an unchangeable future for your children, your loved ones, yourself? Are you locked in a prison of despair, chained to lies that trap you in your past? Jesus came to give new life, to free us and to heal and restore. Our past doesn't have to imprison us. It can be the place where Jesus meets us and sets us on the path to a future of hope.

Dear Father, I ask You to redeem the mistakes of my past and to use them to create a future of hope for others that exceeds what I could possibly envision. Heal wounds, scars, and relationships. Help me to take responsibility for the hurts and mistakes I've caused and to take steps toward reconciliation and healing. Bring wholeness out of the broken pieces and use me, Lord. Amen.

1. What areas of your past are "broken"? Do you feel aspects of your past are irredeemable?

2. What legacy do you believe Jesus envisions for your family? Begin praying for God to move in your heart and the hearts of those around you to accomplish His will in this.

"If Only" Living

Look to the Lord and his strength; seek his face always.

1 CHRONICLES 16:11

In 2010, twenty-three-year-old reality TV star Heidi Montag Pratt surprised American onlookers when she underwent ten cosmetic surgery procedures in one day. Prior to that day, she'd already had a nose job, collagen lip injections, and breast implants. Her reason for subjecting her body to the pain of multiple surgeries? In Heidi's own words, she chose to go under the knife and paid tens of thousands of dollars because she desired to become "the best me."

Many who live in twenty-first-century American culture, like Heidi, find themselves in an endless pursuit of "the best me." Facebook, Twitter, television, and other media show our addiction to chasing the "if onlies" of beauty, sex, power, money, and fame.

If only I looked like . . .

If only I earned . . .

If only I could upgrade to . . .

If only I could fulfill my dream of . . .

If only I could go back and fix . . .

Our "if only" mentality reflects something beyond the cultural idiosyncrasies of our century; it reveals a problem with our hearts, a sin problem. In the Old Testament, we read that God promised Abraham the world would be blessed through his son. When Abraham didn't see results after twenty-five years, he jumped into "if only" thinking and took control of his circumstances. He doubted that God was really going to fulfill His promises, so Abraham reverted to plan B. He decided it would be best if his wife's servant Hagar had a child for him.

As the person who sneaks to open up my Christmas presents the minute after they're placed under the tree, I have to give Abraham credit for waiting twenty-five years. Like him, too often I want my way, and I want it now.

How often are we guilty of taking our eyes off God's plan as we're sucked into "if only" thinking?

If only I didn't have to live with pain . . .

If only things could be like they were before I got sick . . .

If only my friends and family understood me better . . .

If only people really cared about me . . .

"If only" thinking traps us in bitterness. It chains us to regret. It keeps us focused on ourselves and blind to the life God has called us to live—the true "if only" life: "If my people would only listen to me . . . [and] follow my ways . . . you would be fed with the finest of wheat; with honey from the rock I would satisfy you" (Psalm 81:13–16 TNIV).

God promises satisfaction when we trust Him and follow the path He's marked out in His Word—satisfaction at the deepest level of our being and with riches that permanently satisfy. When we feed on the goodness of God and respond to Him in gratitude and obedience, our desires will not be dictated by culture, friends, circumstances, health, abundance, or lack.

But God doesn't force us to listen or follow. Often our hands are to our ears while He's speaking, and the sound of our jabbering drowns out His voice. Like Abraham, we become impatient and head off on a path of our own choosing.

Are you busy chasing dreams of the "best you" today? Or are you pursuing God's "if only" life of satisfaction?

Dear Father, I confess that I've chased after "if onlies" in my life. It's so easy for me to be discontent when I listen to the voices telling me I need to own something or look like someone or measure up to someone's standard. Help me to remember that I need to look into Your face for approval, to seek to please You, and to remember that Your image is stamped upon my life. Amen.

1. How have dreams of "if only"—money, sex, fame, beauty, power—affected your contentment?

2. Read the verses from Psalm 81 above. How would you describe your response to God's call to listen and to obey? Are you experiencing satisfaction in Him?

FedEx Prayers

If that is how God clothes the grass of the field, which is here today and tomorrow is thrown into the fire, will he not much more clothe you— you of little faith?

MATTHEW 6:30 (TNIV)

My friend and business associate Wanda and I were finishing up day twelve of a grueling fifteen-day trip that began with my daughter's wedding near Seattle and ended with a speaking engagement in the Los Angeles County jails. We were exhausted after days on the road, the rigors of the wedding, business commitments, speaking, and the pressures of flying thousands of miles.

My husband, Dan, had been forced to miss our daughter's wedding because of emergency surgery on his eye. I'd cried for days that Jessica wouldn't have her father at her wedding and her dad wouldn't be present to see his only daughter married.

Following the wedding, Wanda and I had blasted down the coast, fulfilling appointments and engagements that left us exhausted. Our final commitment for the trip was to present three sessions in one day to women in the Los Angeles County jails.

Wanda was struggling with an injured knee and would need

a wheelchair to get her from unit to unit within the prison. This meant we needed to locate and rent a wheelchair once we arrived in LA and make arrangements to pick it up. We also needed to mail a box of materials back home to Michigan, pick up dinner, gas up the rental car, and review details for the jail visit the following day. As we inched through LA traffic at rush hour, neither one of us wanted to think about how exhausted we were and how much we had to do before we'd get the chance to rest.

As we headed down the interstate off-ramp and into a business district in the direction of our hotel, I spoke a quick prayer. "Lord, please let there be a FedEx store in the plaza on this corner so we don't have to go searching for one to mail this box. And I'd appreciate it if You could arrange for the medical supply company to deliver the wheelchair to our hotel."

Wanda rolled her eyes at me. "Are you kidding?"

"I'm too tired to be kidding. This is a straight-up prayer of desperation," I answered.

Thirty seconds later, we rounded the corner. FedEx was the first business on the right. And an hour later, I stood in the parking lot of our hotel as a young woman unloaded a brand-new wheelchair from the trunk of her car. "So glad I could help you out by delivering this. Just leave it at the front desk when you're done, and I'll pick it up. We're glad we could give you a deal on the rental rate. We've always wanted to help women in the LA jail."

Sometimes we're reluctant to pray about the small things. We can wrongly think God has bigger problems to take care of and doesn't care about the details of our lives, if we live with chronic illness and pain.

But the Bible tells us that God cares about even the minutia that concerns us. Exodus mentions missing teeth, damages from pyromaniacs, property lines, grazing rights, missing clothes, and borrowing from friends. Matthew 10:30 tells us that even the hairs on our heads are numbered.

Praise God, He cares about the details of our lives, and we can come to Him freely and express our concerns, even if they seem small. He's listening and delights in answering even our FedEx prayers.

Dear God, Your Word shows me You're not bothered or annoyed when I come to You with my requests, whether they be big or small. People once told a synagogue administrator not to bother You with his concerns, but You told the man, "Don't be afraid; just believe" (Mark 5:36). Help me to be persistent in prayer, to give my fears to You, and to pray and believe.

1. Do you ever feel like it's a "waste" to express small concerns to God?

2. Have you ever prayed for something small or unexpected and been surprised by the goodness of God?

USE WHAT YOU'VE GOT

The Lord turned to him and said, "Go in the strength you have and save Israel out of Midian's hand. Am I not sending you?"

JUDGES 6:14

Once again, my friend and business associate Wanda and I were crossing the country on a business trip. We were returning home to Michigan on Amtrak from Sacramento after a weeklong stint in California speaking in prisons, conducting business, and doing radio interviews.

Our funds were limited, so we'd packed food for breakfast, lunch, and snacks and planned to split one of Amtrak's rather pricey evening meals. We also decided to sleep in our seats to avoid the cost of berth rooms, which would have more than doubled the cost of our trip. We chose seats strategically located on the upper level in the center of the car, away from the doors and the stairwell, so we could sleep undisturbed.

A woman about our age boarded at the same time and took the seat across the aisle from us. She carried a plastic bag containing a few baloney sandwiches and a bread bag filled with pork rinds.

Off and on throughout the first day, we tried to engage the woman in conversation, but each time she turned away. When lunchtime arrived, we offered to share our food, but she refused and turned toward the window. That evening, as Wanda and I shared a chicken dinner, the woman munched a thin sandwich. By noon the next day, we noticed that the sandwiches were gone.

Wanda and I didn't have a lot, but we knew we had to share what we had. Wanda dove into her bag and crafted a card with a gracefully lettered Bible verse. We added some cash, and when the lady got off the train at the next stop to smoke, we slipped the card to Kevin, our cabin steward, and asked him to deliver it to the woman anonymously.

Minutes later, she returned to her seat, and Kevin handed her the card. She ripped it open, scanned it, and looked directly at Wanda.

"You! I know it's you." She threw herself across the aisle and into my arms. Then Mary poured out her life story to us. By the time she changed trains in Chicago, we were fast friends. She told us her food had run out and she'd been praying for "just a bit of meat."

It's easy to think that our age, our health, our finances, or our circumstances keep us from ministering to others, but nothing could be further from the truth. God only asks us to use what we have. What's He given to you? You have a wealth of resources:

- *Daily encounters.* Open your eyes to the people God places in your path.
- *Life experiences.* Renew connections with people from your past.
- *Networks.* Determine who can be blessed by other people in your circle of influence.
- *Gifts and talents.* Use your gifts and talents to mentor or serve.
- *Stuff.* Give away your stuff. Or sell it and bless someone with the money.
- *Spiritual maturity.* Share your wisdom. Teach and invest in others and the kingdom of God.

No matter where you are right now, "Go in the strength you have." God is sending you. Ask Him what He may want you to use.

Father, may I be willing to do what I can with all that I have, wherever I am. Give me a willing heart and open hands. Amen.

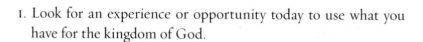

1. Look for an experience or opportunity today to use what you have for the kingdom of God.

2. Make an inventory of things you could use to benefit others, based on the list above. Are you passionate about anything on your list? Pray that God might lead you to future opportunities to serve and minister.

SHARING SPACES

The Lord God is a sun and shield; the Lord bestows favor and honor;
no good thing does he withhold from those whose walk is blameless.

PSALM 84:11

During my childhood years, my father meticulously cared for our home and belongings. And he believed taking care of our possessions was a family affair. Saturdays meant a list of chores for my brother and me: washing and detailing the car, sweeping out the garage and driveway, raking leaves or picking up sticks, washing windows, and what seemed to be countless other tasks. Among other things, my father oversaw the maintenance of our car, checking the tire pressure and fluid levels every weekend, and took care of seasonal chores.

An engineer, Dad delighted in finding new and more efficient ways to do things, such as designing a trailer to tow leaves from the garden to our compost pile, devising a self-steering mechanism for our sailboat, and building creative yard swings that mimicked the motion of riding a horse.

So Dad gave up much of what defined him—much of what had brought him pleasure—when my mother's Alzheimer's meant that he and Mom could no longer live in their home. Our family made the decision that my parents would move in with Dan and me for six months or so, and would stay with my brother Paul and his wife, Sheryl, for the rest of the year.

Dan and I were used to sharing our space. His father had lived with us for nearly five years, and during that time, our adult children had moved home for short periods of time. But my father was facing the adjustments of shared living for the first time.

He was used to calling the shots in his own home: controlling the remote, overseeing the budget, choosing the brand of toilet paper, shooting his BB pistol in the yard, and engineering contraptions for his house. How would we work through the nuts and bolts of living under one roof? It soon became apparent that we needed to understand several important principles:

Respect the differences. My father and I represent different generations. He could teach me about frugality, hard work, and ingenuity. I could teach him to respect elements of the twenty-first century. People who live in shared spaces need to view diversity through the lens of respect.

Set boundaries. My husband is the head of my home, not my father. Certain behaviors are not acceptable in our home, and we needed to negotiate regarding those things. Similarly, I needed to respect my father's need for privacy, honor, and value.

Search for common ground. I granted my father the fullest possible freedom in my home to create gizmos and gadgets. My brother was willing to attend a smaller church that was more manageable for my parents.

Search your heart. It was difficult for my father to transition into a role of dependency. He was forced to give up his home, relinquish his driving privileges, give financial oversight to his children, and place his desires on a back burner for the sake of his family. Although his expressions of love in words may have been sparse, he modeled a life of sacrificial love.

In one way or another, we're all "sharing spaces" in life. May we be quick to model sacrificial love and to lay down what is temporal and slipping through our fingers.

Father, I so quickly forget that I'm only here for a moment, and that life is about learning, releasing, and preparing for eternity. Help me see what I should relinquish and how to grant grace. May I honor those around me and model a life of sacrificial love. Amen.

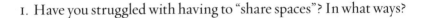

1. Have you struggled with having to "share spaces"? In what ways?

2. How are you learning to model sacrificial love?

Too Young for This?

Don't let anyone look down on you because you are young,
but set an example for the believers in speech, in life, in love,
in faith and in purity.

1 TIMOTHY 4:12

During the Christmas holiday of 2009, thirteen-year-old Chris was an active, healthy teenager, living life full-on. He loved acting, tennis, and being involved in his church youth group.

While he was vacationing with his family, he developed a sudden insatiable thirst. His mother was concerned, but Chris had always been a healthy kid and was going through a growth spurt. She watched him closely for a few days. When it became obvious her son was losing weight rapidly, she scheduled a doctor's appointment.

The doctor's diagnosis came almost immediately: Type I diabetes. Chris had been "lucky." One more day without treatment and he would have required hospitalization.

Chris and his mother were shocked. He knew little about diabetes, but he knew diabetics could die and required shots. At the doctor's words, Chris burst into tears. His mother comforted him, but neither one of them had time to process what they'd been told. They were sent to the hospital, where they spent the next eight hours trying to absorb information about the pancreas, insulin, blood sugar levels, and how to manage diabetes.

Over the following months, Chris learned that juvenile diabetes could be managed, but he struggled with grief and anger at God. No one else in the family had diabetes. Why had God chosen him to suffer with this illness?

After the initial shock, Chris began to accept his diagnosis. Chris says he now views diabetes as a blessing to glorify God and not a curse. His illness has given him amazing opportunities. He's shared his faith on national radio and television. And he's had the opportunity to co-write an inspirational Christian song with Dove Award–winning songwriter Steve Siler. "Crooked Road" is being used to encourage young people and those with debilitating, sometimes incurable illnesses and disabilities across the nation. (Visit http://bit .ly/mpnmBZ to read the lyrics.)

Chris's illness has drawn him closer to God, and as a result, he's grown in his relationships, self-confidence, and ability to reach out and serve others. Since his diagnosis, he's drawn encouragement from the Psalms. Those Scriptures have helped him address his grief, questions, and his deep desire to praise God since his diagnosis.

Today Chris is growing as an actor and taking lead roles on stage. His advice to other young people facing debilitating illnesses?

"Disease doesn't have to cripple you. Expect a period of grieving and questioning. That's normal. But live life as fully as possible with your disease. Your illness doesn't define you; it's secondary to your identity and gifts. Continue to be who you were created to be, to grow in godly character, and to express gratitude."

Lord, we simply do not understand why children have to suffer, and our prayer is always for relief and for healing. But we know You use our illnesses as well, and we pray for opportunities for sick children and young people to bring blessing to others. Help us remember that disease does not have to destroy us and that we can still embrace our identity and our gifts. Thank You for the grace to live with gratitude for the gifts you give. Amen.

1. Have you ever asked "Why me?" regarding your diagnosis or your circumstances? Did you get stuck there or move on?

2. Disease isn't the only thing that can cripple us. What other things have caused you to "get stuck?" How has God's Word and the comfort of His love helped you move forward?

Help, Heartache, and Heaven

But, Lord, 'tis for Thee, for Thy coming we wait,
The sky, not the grave, is our goal;
Oh, trump of the angel! Oh, voice of the Lord!
Blessed hope, blessed rest of my soul!

It is well with my soul,
It is well, it is well with my soul.

The Bible grows more beautiful as we grow in our understanding of it.

JOHANN WOLFGANG VON GOETHE

M y mother's death in 2007 was painful for our entire family. After a long and emotionally wrenching struggle with Alzheimer's, Mom passed away under difficult but oddly gracious circumstances. While being walked through a doorway, she fell backward and hit her head, causing a brain bleed. Ten days later, she slipped away. Rather than having to endure the lingering death of Alzheimer's, Mom was taken to heaven in a way none of us anticipated.

Mom's funeral was a celebration of her life and her Savior. Phyllis Burke loved God, family, music, and laughter, and her funeral reflected those priorities. During the hours of visitation, our family displayed Mom's Bible in her casket, open to Psalm 25:4–5, favorite verses she'd marked in faded ink: "Show me your ways, O Lord, teach me your paths; guide me in your truth and teach me, for you are God my Savior, and my hope is in you all day long."

Just hours after our family returned home from the graveside service following the funeral, I sorted through the bag of personal belongings the funeral director had returned to me—photos and mementos we'd displayed at the viewing. I was surprised to discover

Mom's Bible wasn't in the bag. I quickly placed a call to the funeral home. It was important that we retrieve it, because Dan planned to read from it at our niece Keri's wedding the following week and give the Bible, a treasured family heirloom, to her as a wedding gift.

But my question to the funeral director was met with a prolonged silence, followed by a heart-wrenching response. "Your mother's Bible was in the casket."

"Yes. And I instructed your staff—twice—to take the Bible out before the casket was closed so it could be passed on to family members, since it's one of my mother's most valued possessions."

The conversations among family members that ensued over the following twenty-four hours were awkward and painful, to say the least, as we decided whether to retrieve the Bible or leave it resting with my mother. Suffice it to say that neither option left us feeling comfortable. But I was reminded of two important things during those conversations: my mother was no longer present in that grave, and the hearts of family members are far more valuable than a memento or an "heirloom," even if that heirloom is a treasured family Bible.

My parents had taught me to do more than to treasure God's Word; they taught me to incorporate its truth in my life. We can use the Bible a number of ways to do that. Most Christians understand that the Bible can be used to come to know God and Jesus better as we read and meditate because our heavenly Father reveals himself through His written Word.

Scripture is also our guidebook for life, providing counsel in times of trouble. God's Word is "a lamp to [our] feet and a light for [our] path" (Psalm 119:105). It provides wisdom for the spectrum of life's problems: relational issues, abuse, abandonment, grief, despair, aging, illness—no matter our age, culture, or station in life.

The most important way we can use Scripture is to discover the "mind of Christ" (1 Corinthians 2:16). To know the mind of Christ is to think His thoughts, to share His priorities, to see others as He sees them, and to respond to the world as He would respond. The pursuit of the mind of Christ is a lifetime endeavor that involves study, meditation, discipline, and sacrifice.

"That Christ has regarded my helpless estate and hath shed His own blood for my soul." This is where the mind of Christ begins— with our daily admission of helplessness and acceptance of God's grace, with a commitment to the Word of God that goes beyond paper and ink to a commitment that is etched upon our hearts.

This is the reality of the Word we must live out when Mom gets buried with the Bible and the family fragments. Yes, God's Word is sufficient for even these moments.

The Advocate Advantage

*The heart of the discerning acquires knowledge,
for the ears of the wise seek it out.*

Proverbs 18:15 (TNIV)

M y husband, Dan, and I had served on staff at a small, rural church and Christian school for just over a year when he hired an enthusiastic young graduate fresh out of Bible college to serve as a Bible teacher and athletic coach. Brian's wife, Karen, was a pure sanguine—an attractive, athletic blonde who lit up a room the moment she entered. The moment I met Karen, I knew we'd become fast friends. But it didn't take long for me to notice she often struggled with fatigue and joint pain and avoided going out in the sun.

Karen confided to me that as a teenager, she'd been diagnosed with a systemic form of lupus that can attack the body's major organs and connective tissues and cause life-threatening health problems. She vacillated between periods of remission and "flares" and was frequently on a complex mix of medications.

Over the next eight years that Dan and I worked with Brian and Karen, I read about lupus so I could know how to help my friend.

I learned about her symptoms, her medications and their side effects, the progression of the disease, and lifestyle recommendations. Karen experienced few flares of her disease over those years. My goal was to be an encouragement and sounding board for a friend struggling with a painful, chronic illness.

A year after I met Karen, she became pregnant with twins, which required her to go off her medications for an extended period of time. She took this step after much prayer and deliberation, since stopping her meds put her health at risk. During those months, our church family watched over her, keeping tabs on what she needed and how she felt. Women from our church helped Brian with cooking and cleaning as the symptoms for her lupus worsened. When Karen's twins were born, her lupus went into full flare, and she became too ill to care for them. Two babies were a challenge for a husband caring for a wife who was still extremely ill and exhausted from childbirth. So our family and another church family each "adopted" a twin for a short time, learning how to feed and care for the tiny preemies until Karen was well enough to have them home again.

Karen could have chosen to keep her illness from others. Or she could have refused help. She was young, strong, smart, and athletic; she could have clung to a desire to be seen as competent and the "perfect" mother. After all, what mom would want to place her newborn babies in someone else's hands? But Karen chose what was wise—for herself, for her husband, and for her children.

Karen understood her disease was a medical marathon, and she allowed her church and community to be Jesus' hands for her along the way. She sought and accepted counsel from others. She learned about her illness and developed a network of friends who could offer practical and emotional support when she needed it most. She was wise enough to recognize when she needed help, to accept it, and to move back into a life of independence when she was able. She allowed friends to advocate on her behalf, to "carry her stretcher" at moments when her strength was failing (see Mark 2:1–12), and to extend Jesus' love to her family.

Has God equipped you to be an advocate for others? Or perhaps you, like Karen, need to search out others who can help carry your stretcher during a difficult time. God meets the needs of His people through His people. Is He speaking to you today?

Dear Father, thank You for those You've placed around me to carry me on days when I cannot stand. Father, You've called us to serve one another. Give me a heart willing to accept the love and care of others. May I be willing to ask when I am in need and respond with a heart of grace when I am asked. Amen.

1. Who has served as an advocate in your life? How did he or she help care for your practical needs, serve as a liaison between you and the medical community, or provide spiritual refreshment?

2. Are you in need of an advocate today? Who might that person be? Are you standing in a place where you might be called to serve as an advocate for someone else?

LONGING FOR WHAT HAS BEEN LOST

Joseph said to his brothers, "Come close to me." When they had done so,
he said, "I am your brother Joseph, the one you sold into Egypt! And now,
do not be distressed and do not be angry with yourselves for selling me here,
because it was to save lives that God sent me ahead of you . . . So then,
it was not you who sent me here, but God.

GENESIS 45:4–5, 8

One of my closest friends—a fun-loving woman hovering a bit below the big "Five Zero"—has lived with multiple sclerosis, as well as a number of other debilitating illnesses, for more than ten years. Unrelenting pain attacks her body from her head to her feet, randomly moving from her hands to her eyes to her legs to her back or to other parts of her body. On any given day, she's unable to predict to what degree she'll be able to physically engage with the world.

My friend admits that what she often finds most discouraging about her pain are the "small things" she's lost. Cooking is one of her greatest passions, but it's almost impossible for her to prepare a meal on her own, since she no longer has the strength or dexterity to open jars or lift heavy cooking utensils. She can't remove the caps from her pill bottles. She struggles to pull on boots and shoes. She can walk only short distances. Even though she takes the strongest anti-nausea prescription available, sickness threatens every attempt to go to church, meet friends, drive to the store, work at her computer, eat meals, or even take showers. Plastic bags are never farther away than arm's reach. It's a humbling way to live. And few people know about her struggles. Over the years, she's chosen to keep the details of her illness to herself, rather than to explain the complications and realities over and over again to people who try to sympathize (or maybe don't) but really have no way of relating to her life.

Illness can alienate us from friends, family, and loved ones, and if we're not careful, we can become isolated, angry, and resentful as a result. Joseph, who was betrayed and abandoned by his brothers in the Old Testament, rose to power only to be unjustly accused and thrown into prison. He could have chosen resentment as a response to his circumstances. But, instead, he used even the negative circumstances of his life as a platform to bring glory to God (see Genesis 37–50).

In one way or another, we've all faced the loss of "small things." But those things can become idols if they draw us away from faith in God.

How have you dealt with loss of "small things"? Has resentment seeped into the edges of your life? Ask God to show you ways that you can bring glory to Him in your circumstances, even as you relinquish the "small things" as acts of worship and sacrifices of praise.

Dear Father, I acknowledge that I've been bitter because of the things that I feel I've lost. I've felt entitled to resentment, anger, and a bad attitude. Please forgive me. Help me to see my anger and bitterness as a sin against You. Help me see that I stubbornly rationalize my motives. I submit my will and my intentions to You. May I seek to become more like Your Son, Jesus. Amen.

1. Have you faced diminishment or loss due to illness? What losses have been most difficult for you and why?

2. How do you deal with resentment? Are you still struggling today?

A Time to Weep

There is an appointed time for everything. And there is a time for
every event under heaven—
A time to give birth and a time to die;
A time to plant and a time to uproot what is planted.
A time to kill and a time to heal;
A time to tear down and a time to build up.
A time to weep and a time to laugh;
A time to mourn and a time to dance.
A time to throw stones and a time to gather stones;
A time to embrace and a time to shun embracing.

ECCLESIASTES 3:1–5 (NASB)

The past three years of my life have borne the watermarks of grief: the deaths of parents and close friends, health crises, and challenging life transitions. And with each loss and adjustment, I've felt a tug of guilt regarding the tiny word *joy.* As Christians, we're often told that we should experience joy in the middle of our trials. We can carry the expectation that we must "feel good" when life is excruciatingly painful. But often our emotions don't follow suit. In response to our feelings of discouragement, emptiness, or anger, we may experience feelings of guilt, thinking ourselves unspiritual for not feeling cheerful.

After I lost my mother, I felt a deep heaviness and ache for many months. Two years later, that same feeling still washes over me on a regular basis. Yet, in spite of feeling heartache and sorrow, I never doubted the presence of joy in my life. Joy is the sustaining oxygen of my soul, the hope that flows through my veins and gives me life, even when I'm unaware of its presence. Author Tommy Newberry defines joy this way in *The 4:8 Principle*: "Joy means that you emphatically trust God and believe that he has great plans for your life, regardless of what is happening right now. Joy is an outward sign of inward faith in the promises of God."

Dear friend, pastor, counselor, and author Gary Heim recently responded to the e-mail of a close friend of mine who'd lost a child. She, like many who experience deep grief, was searching to better understand the essence of joy in the months following her son's death.

Gary's words provided a comforting perspective about the heart of God in our times of sorrow:

> In Acts 20, Paul and his friends weep deep tears because he understands he'll never see them again. The "neverness" of not seeing our loved ones' faces again in this life is so painful to us.
>
> The Bible says we will experience times and seasons in life: times to weep and times to laugh, times to mourn and times to dance (Ecclesiastes 3:4). Right now, dear friend, you're in the season of weeping and mourning. Christmas, birthdays, and "turning points" will be especially painful. It's only right to deeply feel the gut-wrenching, soul-tearing loss of your dear son and the shattered dreams you had for

him as a mother. Your tears and grief honor your child; they say his life mattered and you feel his absence deeper than words could ever express.

God puts no pressure on you to feel joy. Perhaps your pain is so nearly unbearable that your soul longs to feel joy, like a drowning person gasps for air, but God doesn't pressure you. Your lack of felt joy doesn't mean you don't love God or trust Him. Our grief can be compared to rain clouds that block the sun—while we may not feel the sun, it is still there, and the same is true of our love for God.

God is love, and love is patient and kind (1 Corinthians 13:4). God is patient and kind toward you in your journey through this valley of the shadow of death. He is with you and will get you through this.

The Bible says that through all the seasons of our lives, God will make everything beautiful, but beauty comes in God's time, and we sometimes don't see it until much farther on our journey (Ecclesiastes 3:11). Believing that there will be joy may feel impossible right now, but be patient with yourself as your broken heart grieves. God's heart breaks with you, and He is holding you.

When I'm tempted to judge my joy by my feelings, I must remind myself that feelings are not a measurement of truth or my standing with God. He wired our hearts for eternal relationships, and we hurt when temporal ties are broken. He compassionately grants grace in our times of grief and places no expectation on us for "right" feelings when we lose those we love. As the Spirit of God carries us in faith in our moments of sorrow, we can trust that joy will come in the morning.

Dear Father God, I admit that at times I do not feel joy. Sometimes the grief threatens to overwhelm me when I think about not seeing the face of my loved one again in this life. But I know I can trust in Your Word and that I can trust in You. I know You have a plan and a purpose—even for pain. No matter what I feel, I choose to trust You. Please heal my broken heart. I thank You for Your loving faithfulness. Amen.

1. Have you ever felt pressured to be happy or joyful when you were going through a time of grief? Did you feel guilty or like you might be disappointing God or others?

2. How would you grant your own child compassion to grieve during a time of painful loss? How do you think this might reflect the heart of our loving heavenly Father?

REFUGE

I will say of the Lord, "He is my refuge and my fortress,
my God, in whom I trust."

PSALM 91:2

For our twenty-fifth anniversary ten years ago, friends blessed Dan and me by taking us on a cruise through the Panama Canal and to South America. We were overwhelmed at the prospect of being treated to an incredible adventure, and I spent months studying ports of call and historic and cultural sites, envisioning what it would be like to actually visit exotic locations I'd only heard and read about.

The four of us embarked from Florida on Halloween. Little did Dan and I know that hurricane season in the Caribbean extends from June through November. As Midwesterners, we'd heard news reports about tropical storms, but we'd certainly never experienced them. That was about to change.

During our evening meal that night—somewhere between the pumpkin soup and beef Wellington—the ship began to rock and then heave as the waves increased to thirty foot swells. I excused myself and haltingly made my way down the shifting hallway back to our cabin. Later that night, I lay in bed gripping Dan tightly, praying we wouldn't be flung to the floor as the ship shuddered against the slamming waves. As I was tossed like a Caesar salad at an Italian lunch, a single thought pounded through my brain: we were helpless against the towering waves, surrounded by miles of surging seas. Our ship was a fleck of flotsam in the midst of the massive expanse of ocean. Our engine strength couldn't compare to the pounding power of the water surrounding us. Our lives depended upon the whim of the next wave. The raging storm offered no means of escape, no place of refuge. Even the ship's captain could have only directed us to a lifeboat and prayed for the best—safety, security, refuge from the storm.

King David faced the fury of raging storms. For years, King Saul sought to kill him, so David took refuge in the hills and caves in Israel. Enemies came against him in battle and plots of intrigue. Even David's own son Absalom turned against him. And in each instance, David sought God as his refuge. In 2 Samuel 22:2–4 we read David's testimony of praise for protection and deliverance: "The Lord is my rock, my fortress and my deliverer; my God is my rock, in whom I take refuge, my shield and the horn of my salvation. He is my stronghold, my refuge and my savior—from violent people you save me. I called to the Lord, who is worthy of praise, and have been saved from my enemies" (TNIV).

No matter the storms we face in life, our only true refuge is God. His love undergirds us like a rock—firm and immovable. C. S. Lewis has said, "Though our feelings come and go, God's love for us does not." As our refuge, God stands as our shield, protecting us from Satan's intentions for us and from the full weight of this world's sin. Everything that touches our lives passes through God's shield of protection. Because of this, even the pain and suffering of this world can be transformed for His good purposes. God also stands as the only source of our salvation and refuge. Nothing humankind seeks can save; nothing humankind offers God can save. The God of the universe alone can offer us refuge and hope.

Where are you seeking refuge? In your own wisdom? In your own strength? In relationships? Power? Wealth? Acclaim?

With open arms, God calls us to refuge: "God is our refuge and strength, an ever-present help in trouble. Therefore we will not fear, though the earth give way and the mountains fall into the heart of the sea, though its waters roar and foam and the mountains quake with their surging . . . The Lord Almighty is with us; the God of Jacob is our fortress" (Psalm 46:1–3, 7).

Thank You, Lord, that You look for ways to show yourself strong on behalf of those whose hearts are loyal to You. You are the everlasting God, the Creator of the universe, and You are my refuge. Thank You for the strength You provide as my rock, the protection You provide as my shield. Thank You for unfailing love that will continue to be lavished upon me, in spite of what I might do. You are my God, and I will trust You until the end. Amen.

1. What does the word "refuge" mean to you? How has God been your refuge in times of crisis?

2. The Lord Almighty is *with* you. How has God made himself known to you? In what ways has He demonstrated His strength on your behalf?

Dependency

For you know the grace of our Lord Jesus Christ, that though he was rich,
yet for your sake he became poor, so that you through his poverty
might become rich.

2 Corinthians 8:9

My sister-in-law Sheryl was the first person in a series of adults who, in 1999, crossed the line of personal privacy and bathed me. Like most people, I took my privacy for granted. But the day I was admitted to the neuro-oncology unit at Detroit Medical Center, personal privacy disappeared like suds sucked down the drain at the end of a relaxing bath.

Sheryl gently sat me up in my hospital bed, and then wheeled me across my room. I squeezed my eyes tight against the dizziness as she rolled me into the cold bathroom.

I remember the bite of the plastic slats as she lowered me onto the shower bench . . .

the chill of the icy floor beneath my feet,
the gagging scent of soap that set my stomach churning,
the splatter of the water on the tile walls,
the sting of droplets hitting my face,

the brush of unfamiliar hands skimming my skin and scrubbing me clean.

Waves of humiliation surged through me as I clenched my eyes against the nausea. Surges of hopelessness. Embarrassment. Fear that the limitations that marked my hours would define my life forever.

Was I grateful that Sheryl was lovingly caring for my needs? Of course.

But was I also overcome by fear that the independent life I'd always known might come to an end? Yes.

Had I lost my faith in the God who promised to be with me in even my darkest hours? No.

But did I feel Him beside me in those moments as I sat cold, naked, and exposed? No, I did not.

Over the next months, Sheryl was joined by nurses, aides, and family members on the list of people who tended to the needs of a body that refused to obey even the simplest commands. I hated the invasion of my privacy by a seeming army of medical professionals and caring loved ones even more than I hated the symptoms of my illness. I hated this new world of dependency and pain. I certainly would never have chosen it.

Yet over the months of my illness, a new realization dawned on me. Jesus *chose* the very things I hated most because of His love for me. He willingly laid down the perfection of deity and *chose* dependency—a life of physical limitation and suffering, a life of frailty and pain, a body subject to disease and age. He chose stomach cramps and toothaches, hunger and thirst, chills and fever, and the agonies of a slow death on a cross. He chose nakedness, humiliation, suffering, and degradation for one reason: He loved me.

According to 2 Corinthians 8:9, He made himself subject to a fallen human body, to the whims of an earthly climate, and the demands of imperfect people so we might become rich through His loss. So we might gain hope in despair. So we might know that an eternal purpose transcends our earthly pain. So we can place our confidence in a Savior who conquered disease, death, and despair to secure our eternal hope and home.

Even in moments when my dignity feels wounded, I can face the limitations of my imperfect body because God has secured every moment of my life and destiny within His plan.

Dear Lord, at times I feel helpless and hopeless because my body and brain no longer work the way they once did. Help me to be thankful that You will use even my dependency to grow Your kingdom and bring honor to Your name. Thank you for those who care for me, and help me to grant them grace. Amen.

1. Have you faced moments of dependency that have caused you to question your value, your purpose, or your future? How did you deal with those challenges?

2. How has Scripture helped you face your fears of dependency? How has God's Word spoken to you?

From Strength to Strength

They go from strength to strength, till each
appears before God in Zion.

PSALM 84:7

Leg pain in the late-night hours often requires me to take a small dose of a non-narcotic pain medication in order to sleep. And while sleep is a good thing, taking this medicine has its downside. Nothing on the label warns that it can make recipients "slow and stupid." While friends safely take large doses of this drug, my metabolism handles the medication quite differently. With just a quarter dose, my speech becomes slurred, my thinking slows, and three plus three can equal a quart. A slug could beat me in a foot race, and at the slightest turn of my head, I fall to the ground. Heaven help me if I'm walking and need to glance to the side while pronouncing my name.

The other night I attempted to walk from the couch to the bathroom—a distance of approximately fifteen yards. I knew my legs wouldn't carry me, so as I rose, I braced myself against a wall and planned my strategy. I grabbed a nearby bookcase, reached for the wall again, and then grasped a sturdy doorframe until I arrived at the security of the bathroom counter. I'd never have made it to the bathroom if I'd not pulled myself from handhold to handhold.

At times, illness and responsibilities take a toll on my strength, and I feel like it's impossible to take the next step. In addition, our fast-paced, me-first world erodes our health, relationships, emotions, and spiritual strength. While I'd like to claim to be a spiritual Wonder Woman, the more truthful picture is that I sometimes struggle with physical and spiritual fatigue.

The psalmist wrote about journeying through life "from strength to strength" (84:8). Some translations of this verse imply that travelers gain more than distance on their journeys; they also gain stamina and gather strength with each challenge. Isaiah 40:31 parallels this idea: "Those who hope in the Lord will *renew* their strength . . . They will run and not grow weary, they will walk and not be faint" (emphasis mine).

But how do we gain strength as we struggle through difficulties? Shouldn't suffering and trials result in weakness, despair, even rejection of our faith?

The secret lies in God's ever-present supply of grace—handholds that allow us to pull forward and pause to gather our strength. According to 2 Corinthians 12:9, God's grace is actually perfected in our weakness: "He said to me, 'My grace is sufficient for you, for *my power is made perfect* in weakness'" (emphasis mine). Our trials pull us forward as we grow and move "from strength to strength" in our faith. God takes our weakness and, in its place, gives us His strength to carry on through the power of His Spirit.

Our own strength will never be sufficient for our problems and heartaches. But God stands waiting to empower us to live beyond the limitations of this life as we turn to Him.

Dear Father, even though we know we are weak, we can rest in knowing You are our strength. May I trust You even in my weakness. Give me grace and the power that will move me forward even in times of pain. Amen.

1. When have you felt fragile and weak? How have you found yourself strengthened in those times?

2. Describe a time when a trial has been a handhold to a stronger faith.

GUILT

Then I acknowledged my sin to you . . .
and you forgave the guilt of my sin.

PSALM 32:5 (TNIV)

During the weeks I laid in Detroit Medical Center, my husband Dan never left my side. His face was the first thing I saw when I awoke in the gray hours of early morning and his footfall the last thing I heard in the quiet blanket of night as he left my room to grab a few hours of much-needed sleep at my brother's home.

Dan stood beside me for every procedure and served as my advocate in every decision. He spooned nourishment into my mouth and bathed my body. He prayed over me and wept with me. He held my hand and bolstered my heart.

And, for the most part, he was applauded for remaining at my side during the long stretch of days when doctors were trying to stop the progression of the unknown disease that was threatening my life. But even in my weakened condition, I sensed after the first weeks that friends and co-workers occasionally questioned how long it would be practical for him to remain at my side. After all, I was an adult, and Dan could actually *do* very little to help me. How long could he stay away from his job without compromising the needs of his employer?

Although I would have been devastated if Dan had left my side, I felt guilty that my illness was tearing him from his job, our children, and responsibilities at home. I felt guilty that my illness was influencing his reputation. I felt guilty when I looked into his weary eyes. As the days of my hospitalization wore on and my condition remained the same, my guilt and feelings of helplessness grew.

But over the ensuing months, God taught me that other people weren't my responsibility. My job was to focus on my heart (more than enough work for a lifetime). For instance, I was responsible for learning the difference between true guilt and false guilt. True guilt stems from moral failure, sin, or wrongdoing. False guilt comes when we try to meet the unrealistic expectations of others.

We must be sensitive to the conviction of the Holy Spirit when we're guilty of wrongdoing, but we also need to build boundaries that protect us from false guilt. Learning to distinguish between true and false guilt has freed me from bondage to inappropriate expectations.

Consider the following checklist as you evaluate guilt in your life:

+ True guilt is based on a violation of God's standards.
+ True guilt is a result of sinning against others.
+ False guilt is a by-product of self-condemnation and an inability to forgive ourselves.
+ False guilt makes us responsible to the unrealistic expectations of others.
+ False guilt makes us feel guilty when we've done nothing wrong.

When I was hospitalized, my faithful husband chose to stay at my side in my moment of need. My guilt stemmed from fearing what others would think.

Have you learned to discern between true and false guilt? Learn to recognize false guilt for what it is: a lie of Satan. Don't allow him to trap you in self-defeat when Jesus so freely offers us life free from the burdens of unrealistic expectation and lies.

Dear Father, thank You that You love me, no matter what I've done or haven't done. Please forgive my sins and give me discernment between true and false guilt. Help me overcome the burdens of false guilt and shame. Thank You that I don't live under a burden of condemnation. In Jesus' name. Amen.

1. Have you struggled with false guilt? How have you dealt with it?

2. Colossians 3:13 tells us to forgive one another, but the Greek word for "forgive" includes forgiving ourselves. Are you living free from the weight of guilt toward yourself? If not, ask Jesus to release yourself from the bondage of unforgiveness.

Learning and Leaning

Search me, O God, and know my heart;
test me and know my anxious thoughts.

Psalm 139:23

For many years of my adult life, I made it my job to run my corner of the world and any other corner I could get my hands on. I was certain I'd figured out the answers to my problems and everyone else's, too. My kids even gave me an embroidered pillow for Christmas one year that summarized my view of life: "I'm not bossy. I just have better ideas."

I'd been raised in a Christian home, gone to a Christian college, and graduated from a respected seminary. Along the way, I'd unknowingly become a judge of truth—someone who has opinions about it but struggles to live it out. But God, in His grace, decided to change that—and a few other things about me.

My illness in 1999 was part of God's plan to slow me down and show me who I really was. In the months I lay bed-bound, I was alone with my thoughts and forced to pay attention to my negative self-talk. I began to recognize that a steady stream of conversation ran through my head—messages about God, about myself, about others, about my circumstances. And many of those thoughts contradicted the Word of God. I began to see that, although I was a Christian, I lived in two worlds: I clung to the belief that I was loving God and others, but I was often living for myself.

God showed me that my self-talk was a powerful gift—the key to intimacy with Him and to my spiritual growth. Over the months following my illness, I studied my thoughts, praying and listening for the Holy Spirit to speak to me. In the promptings of my thoughts, God was calling me to change and to newness of life. I began to "lean into" those moments—listening for God's voice and searching my heart and thoughts for lies I told myself that were in conflict with the Word of God.

Over the past six years or so, the Spirit of God has changed my heart and healed strained relationships with family members. My controlling, manipulative spirit has softened. My critical tongue and harsh tone appear far less frequently, and I'm far more willing to listen to others. My judgmental tendencies have tempered and given way to grace.

Our loving heavenly Father is gracious. He loves us as we are, but He doesn't leave us where He finds us. We're called to a life of constant growth. The Bible calls it sanctification, as we're conformed more and more to the image of Jesus Christ. Self-talk is the secret to intimacy with God as we listen to the whispers of the Holy Spirit and lean into relationship with God and the promise of renewed lives.

Leaning means reaching forward, with my eyes upon a goal. Leaning means I'm willing to place myself in a state of imbalance— to look at myself from a new vantage point that may make me feel uncomfortable. It means living in a state of expected change that's been promised by Jesus himself (Philippians 2:1–11).

My prayer is that I won't be the same person three months or a year from now and that I'll still be listening, learning, and leaning into change.

> *Dear Father, You know the lies that have kept me in bondage, and You know that it's hard for me to let go of them because they can seem so true. But help me choose to believe Your Word above all and to act upon it. Change my heart. May I be sensitive to Your Spirit as I learn to listen and lean in to You. Amen.*

1. What are the greatest lies you've discovered in your self-talk? How do you combat them?

2. In what ways have you changed and grown spiritually in the past two years? How has your self-talk played a part in this?

Never Alone

Be strong and courageous. Do not be afraid or terrified because of them,
for the Lord your God goes with you; he will never leave you nor forsake you.

Deuteronomy 31:6

B y the time she was five, Lisa had become a mother to her young-er brother, protecting him from parents whose addictions made them unable to care for their children. By the time she was seven, her parents had been sent to prison, and she and her brother had been placed in foster care. The system was not kind, and Lisa's feelings of isolation grew.

Along the way, however, God placed people in her life: a loving grandfather who introduced her to Jesus; aunts, uncles, and friends who provided safe havens; teachers and pastors who gave encouragement and hope. But by the time she was an adult, Lisa mistrusted the world and was fiercely independent. She remained single and found success in her job in the media industry. Then, at the age of forty-four, she was diagnosed with multiple sclerosis. The first flare of the disease ravaged her body for months, but she hid her diagnosis from family and friends and continued to work remotely from home. Over the following years, she seldom felt well and isolated herself, not sharing her illness with anyone and sinking further into a depression she'd struggled with since childhood.

Even while running from nightmares of the past, Lisa felt God pursuing her—a God who longed to show His love. When she pulled away from Him, He seemed to press closer. As the months passed, her desperation increased, and she cried out to God for help. She was angry about her life of pain and wasn't sure she could trust a God who had allowed such suffering. But she knew that she was crying out to the loving heavenly Father her grandfather had introduced her to as a child.

Unexpectedly, God answered her prayers and sent a friend into her life, a woman familiar with MS who'd also suffered the pain of abuse. Slowly, Lisa began to understand that God had answered her prayers. He had sent tangible help, and He was asking that Lisa trust Him and begin trusting others.

Lisa began to take steps toward a healthier lifestyle. She backed away from negative relationships and life choices. She began a program of self-care and started working with a counselor. Eventually she reconnected with spiritual mentors and moved out of her life of seclusion and into a new community. She went back to church and began pursuing her love of music and art.

Looking back, Lisa recognizes that God never left her alone. He was beside her in the touch of loving relatives. He reached out to her through redemptive relationships. He rescued her from the brink of despair time and again. Because He is God, His power overcame even the pain of this world to draw her to himself.

God is always with us, whether or not we see it or feel it. He pursues us even in our darkest moments of despair. He is a God of relentless love.

Dear Father, sometimes the pain and suffering of life overwhelms me. At times I don't see You or feel You, and I've struggled to trust You. Thank You for relentlessly pursuing me, even when I don't see You or sense You. Thank You that Your love isn't dependent upon what I can see and understand. Thank You for mercy and forgiveness. Continue to draw me close to You, Lord, for even in my unbelief, my heart knows only how to cry out to You. Amen.

1. Lisa's story offers hope to others who have experienced abuse and suffering. When has God relentlessly pursued you?

2. Did someone teach you about Jesus when you were a child? How did this influence you in later years?

A HEART FOR HEAVEN

Peace I leave with you; my peace I give you. I do not give to you as the world gives. Do not let your hearts be troubled and do not be afraid.

JOHN 14:27

At the age of forty, Nora Bradshaw was diagnosed with a rare form of leukemia. Although doctors administered intensive chemotherapy and performed a bone marrow transplant, the procedures failed. A year later, Nora—a wife and mother—was given just months to live. How did she respond?

Joyfully.

She knew the cancer had returned and she was fighting a losing battle. And although she admits sorrow at leaving her husband and two daughters, Nora's greater focus was on preparing for heaven and what awaited her.

"I believe in miracles, but I also believe God also sometimes has other plans. There's no doubt in my mind He can do miracles, but do I think it's going to happen to me? No. I think I'm going to heaven."

In the final months of her life, Nora focused on her greatest priorities. She planned her funeral and wrote her obituary. She took a final vacation with her husband, and she helped plan her daughter's wedding. Defying doctors' predictions, she felt well enough to not only attend the wedding, but to enjoy the celebration pain-free, in spite of lab reports that indicated she should have been bedridden and unconscious.

Nora also chose to express gratitude in everything. She thanked God that most of her days were comfortable and that she had the freedom to enjoy friends and family. She was even given the opportunity to help lead a final communion service with her church family.

Nora's greatest comfort was thinking about what heaven would be like. "I imagine heaven to be like a beautiful garden of Eden. I think about walking with Jesus, running, and not getting tired. Imagine—no pain and no sorrow. It will be wonderful to lie down by a quiet stream and not get cold or eaten up by bugs."

Some people find Nora's positive attitude remarkable, but she didn't see anything extraordinary about her outlook. As long as friends can remember, Nora had talked about going to heaven. She grasped the reality of her future.

"I'm going to heaven. How can I not be excited? I'm going to rise before my Lord. I'm not going to be sick any more.

"I'd like people to walk away at the end of my funeral praising the Lord. I don't want them to be sad because the day I go to heaven is gonna be a great day."

Dear Father, I'm not certain I would have the faith of Nora Bradshaw if I were given a few weeks to live. But I ask for a peace that passes understanding and a joy that gives purposes to my pain. Thank You for providing victory over the grave through the death of Your Son, Jesus. Amen.

1. How do you envision heaven? Do you find yourself focusing more on heaven as you grow older?

2. What does it mean for you to "die well"?

SECTION 6

Lies, Legacies, and Letting Go

And, Lord, haste the day when my faith shall be sight,
The clouds be rolled back as a scroll;
The trump shall resound and the Lord shall descend,
"Even so"—it is well with my soul.

It is well with my soul,
It is well, it is well with my soul.

We are built for the valley, for the ordinary stuff we are in,
and that is where we must prove our mettle.

OSWALD CHAMBERS

A dozen years or so ago, I was counseling a young woman in one of the schools where Dan and I worked. Lisa was struggling with heart-breaking issues that were her responses to extreme abuse and trauma. I was encouraging her to seek professional counseling and to reconsider unbiblical choices that were resulting in painful consequences.

She was defensive and angry and felt justified in the choices she was making. At one point she leaned forward in her chair as she spit out a question.

"So your God has the power to change my life?"

"Yes."

"And help me stop abusing my body . . . take care of myself and stop doing things that I think make me the way I am, right?"

"Right."

Lisa stuck a finger in my face. "Then how about you stop abusing your body, lose about seventy-five pounds, and get back to me?" She rose and left my office, slamming the door behind her.

Ten minutes later, I'd gathered my composure. I knew Lisa's words had been meant to shift the discussion from her responsibilities to me. But she'd challenged me with sobering truth. If God was big enough to change Lisa, He was big enough to change me, and it was time for me to put my money where my mouth was.

For years I'd believed my weight "trapped" me. This time I decided to stop listening to the lies I'd been telling myself and counter them with truth.

- I was not trapped. God's Word tells me in 2 Peter 1:3 that "His divine power has given us everything we need for a godly life through our knowledge of him who called us by his own glory and goodness" (TNIV).
- God gives us the power to defeat Satan's lies and walk in newness of life: "We demolish arguments and every pretension that sets itself up against the knowledge of God, and we take captive every thought to make it obedient to Christ" (2 Corinthians 10:5).
- I had to act on the truth God had given me. James 1:22–24 says, "Do not merely listen to the word, and so deceive yourselves. Do what it says. Those who listen to the word but do not do what it says are like people who look at their faces in a mirror and, after looking at themselves, go away and immediately forget what they look like" (TNIV).

Lisa's words had reflected back an image of myself I didn't want to look at but needed to change, and I knew I had to move forward in obedience to the conviction of the Holy Spirit.

I'm sad to say I haven't seen or heard from Lisa. I don't know how she's doing. But if we have the chance to meet, she'll see that her words motivated me to become a better steward of my body. I've lost approximately seventy pounds. My diabetic numbers are normal, and I'm off my medications. Her harsh words stirred me to prove that the God I was waving in her face loved me enough to want to work on my heart, too.

We are never too old or too young to change, never too far for God's hand of mercy to reach us, and never beyond the hope of God's redeeming love.

THIRST

"Let anyone who is thirsty come to me and drink. Whoever believes in me,
as Scripture has said, rivers of living water will flow from within them."

JOHN 7:37–38 (TNIV)

It takes a lot for me to lose my composure. On a motorcycle trip through the Badlands in 2002, Dan and I had biked out of the high country near Deadwood on our way to Wall, South Dakota. As we descended out of the mountains, the air temperature climbed to over 100 degrees, and the 115-degree road temperature made heat shimmer off the pavement.

I'd packed several two-liter bottles of water in our side bags, but by the time we arrived at a drugstore, Dan and I had consumed them and poured them over our bodies, and I was delirious with thirst. As I staggered into the store, I spotted paper cups of the elixir of life on a counter in the corner. Approximately twenty people stood in line and sat at tables between me and the water. Little did they know they were in peril of their lives.

I lurched through the crowd, shoving and elbowing as I strategized how to heave them all through the front window to get to *my* water. Of course, I'd like to blame my response on heatstroke. My fragments of memory are a blur . . . but let's just say I got my water, and I got it fast.

Thirst drove me to the brink of desperation that day, perhaps because few things are more important to physical health than water. Between 50 to 60 percent of the adult human body is water. Our lean muscle tissue is approximately 75 percent water by weight, and blood is comprised of 70 percent water. Thirst drives us. Dehydration weakens our bodies and skews our ability to think clearly.

In biblical times, people valued water in ways that are difficult for us to understand today. Life centered on the need for pure water. Nations determined where their cities would be built based on water supply. Families chose land close to wells and rivers. Daily life revolved around the need to obtain and resupply water.

So when Jesus called himself an endless supply of living water in John 7:37–38, he was addressing people's greatest need: undeniable thirst that drives us to something beyond ourselves—the source of life itself.

While it may be difficult for us to think of thirst as a gift, thirst is our invitation to life. It's a reminder that we're dependent upon something outside ourselves—a daily infusion from the Source of Life, Jesus himself.

What are you thirsting for today? Do you feel unloved? Abandoned? Insignificant and invisible? Have you been wounded? Are you bitter about the past or fearful of the future? Jesus calls to us in our thirst, saying, "Come to me." He promises to be the true Source of Life that we seek. Like water to our flesh, He invigorates us through the power of His Spirit and gives us life.

That day I stumbled into the drugstore, my thirst drove me to drink—long, slaking dregs as fast as I could gulp. My thirst drove me to soak up as much water as I could as quickly as I could. I poured refreshing cups on my head and over my arms. I splashed it on my face and neck. I didn't care what I looked like. I felt as if I was dying, and only water would satisfy.

Jesus freely offers everything we need and more as He calls out to us: "Come to me." May we run to Him and accept His free gift of life, refreshment, and hope.

Dear Father, there are times in my life when thirst has come because I've ignored You. But You stand waiting for me with arms wide open to embrace me. Father, may I see my thirst as an invitation to fall into Your arms, to listen for the sweet whisper of Your voice, and to rest in Your love for me. Amen.

1. What does spiritual thirst feel like to you? Has that thirst ever driven you to hopelessness or desperation?

2. Scripture says that Jesus is the way, the truth, and the life (John 14:6). We learn of Him as we meet Him in Scripture, in prayer, and in meditation. How is God calling you to greater intimacy in these areas?

LYING TO MYSELF

Those who listen to the word but do not do what it says are like people who look at their faces in a mirror and, after looking at themselves, go away and immediately forget what they look like.

JAMES 1:23–24 (TNIV)

I tried not to tap my foot as my neurologist asked familiar questions and jotted notes in his file. It was my fifth annual checkup for my brain lesion, and this year it seemed harder than ever to hide my jittery nerves. After my second appointment, I'd figured out that Dr. Barger repeated the same questions. So each year, like a freshman studying for an exam, I'd cram. I'd list the questions and rehearse my answers. Count backward by multiples of seven. Name the past five American presidents, beginning with the current president. Name the parts of a wristwatch. Explain a reading passage.

Every year I went to my exam with a familiar anxiety: What if my score on my assessment dropped? What if Dr. Barger discovered that my unnamed disease had flared to life again? I simply didn't want to face those possibilities.

I was afraid. I couldn't control my responses when Dr. Barger tapped my knees to check my reflexes, poked my limbs with a safety pin, or asked me to walk heel-to-toe down the hallway and I wobbled. I couldn't control what he'd find when he checked my eyes or my fine motor skills. And I couldn't control the results of my MRI. But I *could* control my answers to the questions he repeated year after year. So each year as I left my appointment, I'd jot down as many questions as I could remember. By my fifth annual exam, my list was practically complete.

But I could deceive myself only so long. Six years into my recovery, I finally accepted that I was afraid to face my illness. As long as I toyed with the truth, I'd never be able to face my future.

Today I no longer cram for my neuro exams. I've gotten more comfortable with the fact that I have a neurological disease—several, in fact. (Trust me, I'm not bragging.) I stay informed about my illnesses, but I don't read everything on the Internet, either. I've come to grips with the fact that I'm getting older and my symptoms may increase as I age.

Although at times I still struggle with fear, I've chosen to trust the God who created my DNA and counted out my genes before the foundations of the world. I'm safe in His arms and can trust Him to order my days.

Dear Father, my fears make me lie to myself and hide behind half-truths. Help me to trust Your character and Your love for me and to face the future with confidence, knowing You hold my future in the palm of Your hand.

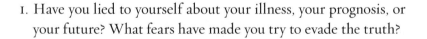

1. Have you lied to yourself about your illness, your prognosis, or your future? What fears have made you try to evade the truth?

2. What truth in Scripture can help you counter your fears? Consider Psalm 103:8–17; 119:37; 139:2–6; Proverbs 13:9; Isaiah 46:9–11; Mark 10:18; and John 14:6.

A Place for Grace

God is able to make all grace abound to you, so that always having all
sufficiency in everything, you may have an abundance for every good deed.

2 Corinthians 9:8 (NASB)

Today my tongue is on fire.

The burn also sears the right side of my mouth and cheek with the intensity of a branding iron. On "good" days I can shove the sensation beneath the surface of my awareness, along with the numbness, tingling, and shooting pain that meander through my arms and legs. On "bad" days the pain claws its way into my thoughts, along with the headache that's pounded my skull since the day my head exploded in a kaleidoscope of pain in 1999.

My body announces my "bad" days to the world. My left eye droops to half-mast—beyond its usual lazy sag—and my left leg drags behind me like a boat anchor. When I'm at my worst, my gait can resemble a toddler whose bottle has been spiked with over-sugared Kool-Aid.

On "bad" days, I struggle to see past my pain. When Dan moves into my line of fire, my frustration and anger tell me to snipe at him. When a friend calls, envy tells me to compare my broken and battered body to her healthy one. When I rifle through the mail, bitterness causes me to resent the bills from hospitals, emergency rooms, neurologists, and labs. And on days when I'm due for a dreaded blood draw and my veins roll and collapse as the phlebotomist misses—for the second and third and fourth time—I fight the urge to take aim and fire with my scorched and searing tongue.

What stops me in those moments when anger surges through me? What gives me the power to serve when I'd rather demand something for myself?

One thing: the knowledge that, although I've done nothing to deserve it, I'm the recipient of God's grace. Moment by moment, I'm given the opportunity to worship Him and extend the grace He's freely given me to others. A thousand times a day, I have the opportunity to worship God by relinquishing my life in acts of obedience and grace, rather than bowing to the god of myself.

For instance, when my husband tracks mud on a clean kitchen floor, and I'd like to shoot him a little attitude.

Or when I'm forced to wait at the doctor's office for an hour and a half, and I miss lunch with a friend.

Or when I'm weary at the end of the day, and a store clerk offers a condescending sneer.

In those moments of irritation and anger, I can choose to make a place for grace. I can choose blessing. I can choose kind words. At times, I can choose to simply smile, stay silent, and lift up a prayer as I walk away.

Like Jesus, I can lay down my rights to retaliate and refute. I can relinquish what I think I deserve and instead choose grace. Recalling the grace that's been given to me, I can choose grace only if my desire to give overwhelms my need to get what I want, when I want it.

The key to giving grace is found in the words of the old hymn:

"When I survey the wondrous cross . . . my richest gain I count but loss."

My prayer each day is that my heart will be so filled with the wonder of Jesus' love and sacrifice for me that I'm left with no room for my selfish desires.

> *Dear Father, I want to make more space for grace in my life. I struggle in moments of anger and frustration and pain, and selfishness tells me to lash out and retaliate. But You tell us to lavish grace and love on even our enemies. I'm so grateful for all Your Son did for me at the cross. I offer you a heart that desires to be like Jesus, merciful and gracious. Amen.*

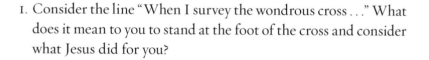

1. Consider the line "When I survey the wondrous cross . . ." What does it mean to you to stand at the foot of the cross and consider what Jesus did for you?

2. In what ways can you make a place for grace in your life?

GOD'S PRESENCE

The Lord stood at my side and gave me strength . . .

2 TIMOTHY 4:17

Several years ago while touring Italy, I visited Rome and the Mamertine Prison, which consists of two underground cells located near the Forum. This prison housed the Roman Empire's most notorious criminals. It's believed to be the jail where Peter was incarcerated before his execution. It's also thought to be the location where Paul wrote 2 Timothy, during his second imprisonment of Nero's reign. During his first imprisonment, Paul was confined to an honorable house arrest, but during his second incarceration, he was held at the dreaded Mamertine. Most Christians were too afraid of ruining their reputations to visit Paul at the Mamertine, if they were able to discover he was there. Prisoners' locations weren't made known, and 2 Timothy 1:16–17 tells us that Onesiphorus— who was brave enough to visit Paul—had to search diligently to find him. Second Timothy 4 tells us that Luke also spent time in the Mamertine prison ministering to Paul.

The Mamertine was notorious for more than its criminals; it stank of human rot. Prisoners and guards alike were tortured by its dampness, especially those confined to the underground chamber. Prisoners were thrown into the lower cell through a hole in the floor of the cell above, and a stone is on display where Peter's head reportedly slammed into the floor after being shoved through the hole above. History tells us that prisoners confined in the lower cell were often chained to a central pillar, where they were starved or strangled.

Paul was intimately acquainted with physical suffering. In 2 Timothy 4, Paul writes that he knows his life is coming to an end and asks Timothy to come quickly and bring his cloak to shield Paul from the dampness of his cell. Paul also knew the pain of abandonment. Demas, Crescens, and Titus had deserted Paul (v. 10). Alexander had been openly hostile to Paul's teaching and may have contributed to his arrest (vv. 14–15). As a final blow, no one showed up to support Paul at his first defense hearing (v. 16); his so-called friends played it safe and deserted him.

Yet Paul is clear about his source of strength: "The Lord stood at my side and gave me strength, so that through me the message might be fully proclaimed and all . . . might hear it . . . The Lord will rescue me . . . and will bring me safely to his heavenly kingdom. To him be glory for ever and ever. Amen" (vv. 17–18). Even as Paul sat chained to a post in the squalid darkness of the Mamertine Prison, he renewed his hope because he was confident that God was with him.

Acts 16:25 tells us that when Paul and Silas were imprisoned together, they praised God by singing. They understood that praise grants believers entrance to God's presence. Their focus was on God's character and promises, not their circumstances or problems. Even as Paul sat in the depths of the Mamertine, he experienced God's power to forgive those who'd abandoned him and proclaim hope to fellow prisoners and his guards.

Do you believe your circumstances hinder God's presence in your life? Then be encouraged by Paul's words, penned in the foul darkness of the Mamertine Prison: "according to the promise of life that is in Christ Jesus . . . grace, mercy, and peace . . . I thank God, whom I serve."

Lord, help me trust You to stand with me when I have no strength, to weep with me when my friends cannot be found, to fight for me when I have no energy. Help me to trust Your presence when I can see only darkness around me so that Your Word might be proclaimed. Amen.

1. Do you believe your circumstances can hinder the presence of God in your life? Why, and in what ways?

2. How has God shown himself to be present in your life in your "dungeon" experiences?

Making God Famous

I will praise thee, O Lord my God, with all my heart:
and I will glorify thy name for evermore.

Psalm 86:12 (KJV)

As a field day volunteer at the end of the school year, Amanda watched as seven-year-old Johnny, third oldest of her five children, ran toward her with a juice box in his hand. His head tilted strangely to one side as he stumbled, and then fell. She made a note to call the doctor. Later that evening the family of seven climbed into their van and stopped for a pizza before heading off to Johnny's baseball game. While seated at the restaurant, Johnny turned in his chair and tumbled to the floor.

Johnny was their most coordinated child—riding a skateboard at one year and learning to roller skate at eighteen months. This wasn't like him. Amanda reaffirmed her decision to call the doctor. But at Johnny's ball game later that evening, her fears eased. For the first time that season, Johnny hit a line drive and rounded the bases, scoring a run for his team.

The following day Amanda called the doctor and explained Johnny's symptoms. Thirty minutes later he was evaluated, and the doctors immediately scheduled an MRI. Neither Rob nor Amanda was prepared to hear the doctor's diagnosis: brain stem cancer, an inoperable form called diffused intrinsic pontine glioma (DIPG).

That night emotions crashed in on everyone. For the first time, Amanda and Rob saw how sick Johnny had been trying not to be. Amanda told her son how proud she was of his bravery and that it was all right to be scared. She read him the story of Gideon and explained that God used unlikely people to lead others, and that Johnny could be like Gideon. She inserted Johnny's name in the story in place of Gideon's name, explaining that he was a mighty warrior who fought bravely so that everyone could know about God. Johnny fell asleep that night with the story of Gideon planted in his heart.

During his treatment at St. Jude Children's Research Hospital in Memphis, Johnny became known as "Johnny the Brave" because he reflected the life of Gideon. Thousands of followers came to know about his courageous battle through television, radio, newspaper, and Internet stories and on Facebook, where his parents, friends, and relatives shared updates.

Eventually eight-year-old Johnny became blind, deaf, paralyzed, and isolated from the outside world. Just before he lost his ability to talk, he was asked if he wanted God to heal him. With slurred speech, he answered, "Yes, I want to be healed."

"Why do you want to be healed, Johnny?"

"Because I want to make God famous."

Before Johnny's death, his story resonated across the world. He met President George W. Bush, and his story was told as far away as India. Johnny was present to open a session of the Arkansas State Legislature. As ball boy for the Cornerstone University basketball team, he served as the inspiration for their 2011 national basketball championship. The V Foundation for Cancer Research, in collaboration with sportscaster Dick Vitale, awarded a 2011 cancer research grant in the name of Johnny Teis. And in celebration of Johnny's ninth birthday, the Teis family partnered with volunteers across the country who performed hundreds of acts of kindness in Johnny's name and handed out hundreds of cards in his memory—an idea born out of Johnny's desire to "make God famous."

In spite of cancer, blindness, deafness, paralysis, and impending death, Johnny Teis lived out his goal.

Today Johnny is healed and whole, in heaven with Jesus. He was granted his desire to make God famous. His legacy is at work in the lives of thousands who were impacted for eternity.

Dear Father, at times I don't feel brave or courageous. I need Your help, dear God. Give me courage to fight in Your strength as I struggle against depression, fear, exhaustion, anger, and doubt. Give me courage to persevere, and strengthen me with Your love and grace for the struggle ahead. Amen.

1. Can you think of a time when a seemingly insignificant act has made God "famous"?

2. Do you believe that to "live is Christ and to die is gain" (Philippians 1:21)? What do those words mean to you?

Retirement

*However, I consider my life worth nothing to me; my only aim is to finish
the race and complete the task the Lord Jesus has given me—the task of
testifying to the good news of God's grace.*

ACTS 20:24 (TNIV)

My husband Dan recently hit his sixty-fifth birthday (incidentally, Dan is *much* older than I am), and our mailbox has
been inundated with insurance offers, senior community advertisements, Social Security information, and AARP mailings. Everyone
seems to be offering advice regarding what retirement should look
like.

Television and movies tell us we should be striving for a yacht in
the Caribbean, where we can collect seashells, play golf, and read to
our heart's content. As those with chronic illness, we may be tempted to think about a point in our lives when we can take a backseat
and coast. But should recreation and self-indulgence mark the culmination of our life goals? We who live with pain have unique wisdom and insight to offer the world.

John Piper, author of *Desiring God* and pastor of Bethlehem Baptist
Church in Minneapolis, Minnesota, notes that the concept of retir-

ing isn't presented in Scripture. He believes retirement should be a time when we invest our talents for God in creative and new ways that leverage the wisdom we've acquired in our previous years of life (www.desiringgod.org/resource-library/ask-pastor-john/should-i -invest-for-retirement). Piper suggests the following principles:

- *Put a governor on your life.* In other words, reject the world's consumer mentality and learn to live modestly and within your means.
- *Make as much money as you can.* Money is not evil, but the love of money is. Make money so you can invest it for God's kingdom.
- *Give as much money as you can.* We make money so we can use money for God's purposes. We're not investing in the kingdom of God if we're simply hoarding.
- *Save what you need to save in order to be a responsible non-borrower.* Avoid buying on credit. Refuse to owe, and learn to leverage the money you do have to *earn* money for you.
- *Retire with a minimalistic plan that frees you to invest in a ministry for the remainder of your life.* Pack light in your retirement years. Live in a way that frees you to invest in ministry and in others. As someone who has experienced pain or chronic illness, you can offer unique life perspective and wisdom. The Internet has expanded possibilities for mentoring, teaching, writing, and networking.

Our life experiences and resources are tools to be invested. A friend of mine who is a former missionary used her love of sewing and ability to interact with non-native speakers to begin a sewing club for Ugandan women. The group started with a handful of women and doubled after the first week. The women—who spoke several different dialects—felt a sense of community among their peers and felt the loving presence of Christ reflected by my friend.

Her sewing club created opportunities to get to know women personally and to share the gospel.

Another friend named Steve—a man in his early fifties—was in a car accident that left him in a wheelchair in a rehab hospital and eventually a nursing home. Over time, it became obvious that he would never return to his job, and he would require residential care indefinitely. Steve contacted his church and asked if they could supply him with copies of inspirational DVDs that would help him connect with others and provide opportunities to tell his testimony for Jesus Christ. Steve's goal was to share the message of Jesus with every resident.

God has gifted us all with unique talents and life experiences. As those who have experienced suffering, we have a unique platform for speaking into the lives of others. When we use our gifts strategically to meet needs, we influence the future for generations to come.

Father, help me to balance my desire to prepare for retirement with a generous spirit. Let me avoid hoarding or believing that I need to live a life of ease in my later years. May I be preparing even now for the ministry You have for me then. Help me to transition with wisdom and grace. Amen.

1. How closely do you follow the principles Piper suggests?

2. Do you feel that the temptations of consumerism draw you? How do you fight against this popular mind-set?

LEGACY

Even when I am old and gray, O God, do not forsake me, until I declare Your strength to this generation, Your power to all who are to come.

PSALM 71:18 (NASB)

At the age of thirty-nine, Jeremy would have been the last man in the world to ponder his life legacy. Life in the fast lane was good. He'd married his high school sweetheart, Allison, and they had two beautiful sons. In spite of a slow California economy, his workaholic efforts had paid off, and his insurance business was thriving. A free-climber and outdoorsman, he regularly headed to Yosemite. And his health was good.

Or so he thought, until he began experiencing stomach pains and weight loss. His doctor's words came like a punch in his sore stomach: pancreatic cancer, with a limited likelihood of cure.

At the age of thirty-nine, Jeremy faced his legacy, and he didn't like what he saw: a veneer of success that hid dark secrets. Recently his wife had discovered his decades-old struggle with pornography. Remorse and shame had shrouded his soul for years, but he'd been unable to break free from his addiction. Now, facing a cancer diagnosis and a prognosis of just months to live, he cried out to God for help.

Jeremy, like many of us, was trapped by a lie. He believed he was chained to his past and had no control over his future or his legacy. But God answered Jeremy's prayers and brought a friend into his life who shared with him truth and hope:

- Nearly 50 percent of Christians, including pastors, report that pornography is a major struggle in their home.
- 42.7 percent of Internet users view porn.
- 53 percent of Christian men attending Promise Keepers events report viewing porn within the last week (www.xxxchurch.com/men/stats.html).

Porn addiction is one of the most difficult addictions to overcome and must be battled on multiple fronts. With the help of accountability and resources and through the power of God, men and women can find freedom from their struggle with pornography. Families can be healed. Marriages can be restored. Lost legacies can be reclaimed.

Jeremy's pastor offered the gift of safety. He also offered mentoring and accountability. He directed Jeremy to resources like Covenant Eyes Internet Accountability and Filtering (www.covenanteyes.com) and the Somebody's Daughter video presentation (www.somebodysdaughter.org).

Over the months that followed, Jeremy prayed about the good and the bad choices of his life and the legacy he would leave as a father and husband. He repented, asked his wife's forgiveness, and agreed to counseling. But he knew words would not be enough. He courted Allison all over again, and their relationship slowly healed. He wrote letters to his sons and his co-workers. As the cancer progressed, Jeremy prepared a videotaped testimony for his funeral and for the young men in his church youth group. He met with leaders from his church and asked them to organize a support system that would help care for Allison during his illness and beyond.

After thirteen months, Jeremy lost his struggle with pancreatic cancer. But he died grateful for the opportunity to heal the wounds of his past, renew his commitment to God, invest his experiences, and re-create a legacy of hope for his wife, his sons, and his community. Like David in the Old Testament, Jeremy reminds us that we are not defined by our failures but by hearts that are sensitive to the Spirit of God.

Dear Father, You know I fail over and over, and I come to You admitting that I have no power of my own to pull myself out of a pit of moral, sinful failure. Yet You sent Your Son to save me, and You see me through mercy's eyes. May I invest in things that last, in building relationships. Give me discernment to see where I need to take steps to begin healing and to take responsibility for reconciliation and repayment of anything I owe. May I leave behind a legacy of love and grace that points to You. Amen.

1. How would you describe your legacy? In what ways would you like to change it?

2. David was a man who failed morally, yet he was a "man after God's own heart" (1 Samuel 13:14). In spite of our failures and shortcomings, how can we leave behind a legacy of faith?

OUR GREATEST FEARS

Peace I leave with you; my peace I give you. I do not give to you as the world gives. Do not let your hearts be troubled and do not be afraid.

JOHN 14:27

I wish I could say I exuded "the peace of God that passes all understanding" (Philippians 4:7) during the weeks when I was first diagnosed with my brain lesion. But, frankly, if I claimed I felt peaceful and unquestioningly spiritual as my body was rapidly disintegrating, I'd be lying.

Instead, I was in shock. One day I could walk, and the next day I couldn't. On Tuesday, I was leading a dozen students through the streets of London. On Thursday, my husband was carrying me. At the beginning of the week, I could calculate international exchange rates as fast as I could spit out my phone number. By Friday, I was lucky to be able to count to three.

All these changes upset my spiritual equilibrium. The things I'd always counted on—my health, my intellect, my ability to navigate through life—were slipping away.

And I was afraid.

Afraid I'd never walk again. Afraid I'd never stop vomiting.

Afraid I'd never be able to read again. Afraid of a dreaded diagnosis. Afraid of a life of pain. Afraid I'd be put on a ventilator, and once they put me on, I'd never come off. Afraid I'd never know what was wrong with me. Afraid I'd never teach again. Afraid I'd lose the life I'd always known. Afraid Dan would be "stuck" caring for an invalid for months . . . years . . . perhaps forever.

I knew Scripture had a lot to say about fear. In fact, the Bible mentions fear approximately 365 times (depending on which translation you're reading). God knows we all struggle with fear and had a lot to say to us about it.

Fear can be a healthy emotion that warns us of danger. For instance, when my son Nate was small, I tried to teach him to fear what could happen to him if he jumped off our garage roof. But fear can also overcome us, disrupt our lives, paralyze us, keep us from thinking clearly, or trap us in depression or negative thinking.

The apostle Paul describes the struggles we face with fear and worry:

> We do not want you to be uninformed, brothers, about the hardships we suffered in the province of Asia. We were under great pressure, far beyond our ability to endure, so that we despaired even of life. Indeed, in our hearts we felt the sentence of death. But this happened that we might not rely on ourselves but on God, who raises the dead. (2 Corinthians 1:8–9)

Surprisingly, God doesn't condemn us because we feel fear. He, more than anyone, knows our struggles. Fear is our invitation to turn to Him for comfort, wisdom, and guidance.

So how should we handle fear? First, we should talk to God. He's waiting to hear from us. We can cast our cares on Him, because more than anyone, He cares for us (1 Peter 5:7). Second, we can rest in the Lord and wait for answers, even in the midst of our circumstances, though answers may not come when we want them or be what we expected. Third, we can do something. While we don't need to fret about small things, we can act on issues that need attention and refuse to dwell on what we can't control. Fourth, we can seek counsel regarding "strongholds" of fear and ask for prayer, accountability, and encouragement. Finally, we can focus on living one day at a time, and if need be, one moment at a time.

Fear is our opportunity to draw close to God. It's our invitation to approach His "throne of grace" where we find our only true source of help—in Him (Hebrews 4:16).

Dear Father, I don't want to confront my fears. The possibilities facing me seem frightening. But I know that You hold the universe in Your hand, and when I can't trust circumstances, I can choose to trust You—not based on my feelings, but on Your Word. Guide me with the truth of Your Word, Father, when I can't see the next step. I place my confidence in You. Amen.

1. How has fear pushed you further from God or drawn you closer to Him?

2. What does it mean to you to "receive mercy and find grace to help" in your time of need (Hebrews 4:16)?

HOSPICE: A MATTER OF HONOR

There is surely a future hope for you, and your hope will not be cut off.

PROVERBS 23:18

Even though my mother had been diagnosed with Alzheimer's for over five years, some of my family members still found it difficult to accept that Mom was facing a terminal illness. The first time I mentioned the word *hospice*, a few relatives packed up their emotional bags and headed for the hills. Their reactions were understandable. To some people, the word *hospice* means one thing: death. It can be difficult to move beyond the word itself to the truth: hospice offers terminally ill patients the opportunity to live out the end stages of their lives honorably and to their fullest.

Hospice is perhaps the most important resource families can access to ensure that their loved one's desires and needs will be met. The criterion for engaging hospice typically requires that one must be diagnosed with a terminal illness that would mean the end of life within six months if the disease progressed at a typical rate. To be eligible for hospice, patients cannot be under treatment to cure the diagnosed illness. A physician must write a referral for a patient to be evaluated for hospice status. If a patient exceeds the six-month term, they can be reevaluated for reinstatement as a hospice patient. Patients who improve can be released from hospice care.

Both my mother and my father-in-law were under hospice care for more than six months. The excellent care they received most likely extended not only the length of their lives, but the quality of their lives.

Our families received irreplaceable resources through hospice. For instance, hospice petitioned for Dan's father, Norman, to be moved to a private room at the veteran's facility, where our family could freely pray, read Scripture, play music, and stay with Norman through the night. Hospice workers also helped my father better understand the emotional, physical, and psychological changes caused by my mother's Alzheimer's.

Hospice workers educated us about Mom's illness and the changes we could expect, helped us understand our ongoing grief, offered resources, explained choices and options, and counseled us as we faced difficult decisions. But most importantly, they understood every aspect of our loved ones' illnesses—and not only the physical ramifications of death, but also the emotional, spiritual, and psychological aspects. They helped us talk through sensitive end-of-life choices, such as feeding tubes, Do Not Resuscitate Orders, and advance directives.

In the final days of my mother's and Norman's lives, hospice workers helped my family find closure and encouraged us to sit with our loved ones, to reminisce, laugh, cry, pray, read Scripture, speak words of appreciation, and honor our loved ones in their final moments of life.

Hospice provides cups of cold water to thirsty families at the end of the long caregiving journey and extends Jesus' arms of compassion to those who are nearing death. But, ultimately, hospice does not help us die. We do that alone. No one can go with us, and even in our final days here on earth, no one can give us peace. Theology is of no use if we have not internalized its reality.

You and I are here on earth to be stewards of our life experiences. When we're done, God has something better for us. When we understand that, heaven takes on a new reality. We understand that we're headed home, and hospice is a threshold as we transition from this place to eternity. Death does not hold a threat; it holds a promise.

Preparing to die means coming to an understanding of life's purpose and the promise of our future in heaven.

Dear Lord, I know I may face pain and suffering in my final months and days on this earth. Please give me wisdom as I make decisions. Some things are easy to discern, and some are challenging—medical complications, financial decisions, decisions regarding what will happen after I'm gone. Give me strength and discernment. Help me see Your truth in every situation. Provide godly counsel, and help me to rest in the counsel You offer. Thank You for providing all that I need, far beyond what I can see in the present moment. Amen.

1. Have you thought through end-of-life choices and made your wishes known in writing? If not, consider doing so as soon as possible.

2. What steps can you take to ensure that your final wishes are honored in both practical matters and in your relationships with family and friends?

LETTING GO

There is a time for everything, and a season for every activity under heaven:
a time to be born and a time to die, a time to plant and a time to uproot.

ECCLESIASTES 3:1–2

My father is an independent, self-made man. He was born the youngest of ten children to immigrant parents and was raised during the Great Depression. From the time he was fourteen, my dad was never without a job. While he was still in high school, he walked into an engineering firm and offered to work for free in order to prove himself. He was hired within the week. During World War II, he served in military intelligence alongside General Eisenhower. And during his career in the automotive industry, he become one of a handful of elite consultants, traveling the globe to troubleshoot and problem-solve for Detroit's top automakers.

As I grew into adulthood, I feared the years when my father would require greater dependency. Dad had always been the family Answer Man, doling out advice to his children and grandchildren, friends and neighbors, and even startled strangers. How would my father respond when my brother and I began offering advice as Dad aged and required increasing assistance?

Those years came sooner than my family expected, as my mother began her struggle with Alzheimer's and my father frayed around the edges as he tried to handle the stress of her emotional and physical changes. It became obvious to my brother and me that Dad needed help.

My trips from Iowa to Michigan became more frequent. One evening as I was preparing to return home, my father collapsed, weeping, in my arms. His concerns for my mother poured out as if a dam in his soul had burst. I assured him he didn't have to care for Mom alone—that our family would provide every support we could find if he would just accept our help.

My dad took an enormous step that night: he admitted he needed help. He allowed my brother and me to formulate a plan—not a perfect plan, but a good one, one we devised with the counsel of pastors, lawyers, doctors, and social workers, and one that respected the wishes of my parents.

Although it was difficult for him, my father began to listen to the advice of his children. He decided to trust us to make wise decisions on his behalf, and with his commitment to trust, he began to relinquish control in select areas of his life. (At the age of ninety-one, my father still writes some of his own checks and controls many of his decisions.) Because of his trust, we were able to consult with lawyers, draw up needed papers, transition Dad and Mom into the best possible living facilities, and make wise financial and medical choices for their long-term benefit.

Over the next years, Dad graciously relinquished his driver's license at his doctor's recommendation. He chose to accompany my mother when we moved her into a home that specialized in dementia care. He willingly laid down his independence to remain at her side until she passed away—an act of Christlike grace and love.

Letting go freed my father to embrace the things most precious to him until the end: keeping his wife and family near him and stewarding the assets he'd worked so hard all his life to acquire. He taught me that letting go can empower us to fulfill our God-given desires if we do so with wisdom and godly counsel.

Dear Father, You know I'm drawn to power and control. Help me see where I need to relinquish control to others in order to best honor and serve You. Give me wisdom to know how to adapt to new seasons of life and new circumstances. Give me godly discernment to know who to trust and when to trust, and to be grateful for the things of the past while leaning into Your promises for the future. Amen.

1. Is it difficult for you to transition into new places and situations in life? How have you learned to lean on God in order to "let go" and move forward?

2. Do you fear trusting others? Why? What does God's Word say to you about those fears?

Appendixes

Appendix I

FIVE STEPS TO TAKE AFTER YOU'VE RECEIVED YOUR DIAGNOSIS

1. **Contact the national foundation or organization that supports those living with your diagnosed illness.** Familiarize yourself with their website and ask for brochures, information, and referrals to support groups in your area. If you're not ready to absorb the information yet, begin a file you can refer to later.

2. **Know when it's not beneficial for you to read about your disease.** The Internet is an endless source of information about the cure, progression, and treatment of diseases. While it's important for you to be aware of symptoms and to know where you can find helpful information, don't read everything about your illness. Much of the information you come across won't apply to your situation and could conflict with your doctor's advice. Use caution and discretion.

3. **Remain hopeful.** New scientific discoveries are continually being made, and medical and pharmacological innovations may influence how your illness is treated. Never assume your illness will win. A positive outlook profoundly affects one's prognosis.

4. **Find advocates who can serve as emotional and spiritual sounding boards.** An advocate could be a pastor, mentor, nearby friend, or phone or online buddy. He or she must have the qualities of a good listener, providing an oasis from judgment and needing to "fix" the things you express. You can find advocates who understand your diagnosis at local support groups or other support environments such as HopeKeepers, a unique Christian small group for those who live with illness or pain.

   Are you refreshed by talking with a friend one-on-one over coffee? Or are you homebound and is signing on to a website more convenient for you? Remember, what works best for you now may not meet your needs down the road. Be willing to make adjustments as your life changes.

5. **Evaluate your personality and patterns of coping.** Ask yourself, "What strengths can I draw from that will help me? Am I a good delegator, or do I need to find a friend to come alongside me to help fill in the gaps? Am I a procrastinator, or am I good at managing the tasks associated with caring for myself and others? Am I a problem-solver, or do I look to others to help me think through strategies? Consider asking a friend or family member to help you inventory the strengths you can leverage, and use those insights to help create a plan.

Appendix 2

RESOURCES

Books: Chronic Illness

Adamson, Kate, *Paralyzed but Not Powerless: Kate's Journey Revisited* (Redondo Beach, CA: Nosmada, 2007).

Beach, Shelly, *Precious Lord, Take My Hand: Meditations for Caregivers* (Grand Rapids: Discovery House, 2007).

Copen, Lisa, *Beyond Casseroles: 505 Ways to Encourage a Chronically Ill Friend* (San Diego: Rest Ministries, 2005).

———, *Why Can't I Make People Understand? Discovering the Validation Those with Chronic Illness Seek and Why* (San Diego: Rest Ministries, 2004).

Hoyt, Dick, and Don Yaeger, *Devoted: The Story of a Father's Love for His Son* (Cambridge, MA: Da Capo, 2010).

Ninteau, Sherrie, *Rick's Story: The Story of Rick Hoyt* (Herndon, VA: Mascot, 2009).

Wallace, Wendy, *Doing Well at Being Sick: Living with Chronic and Acute Illness* (Grand Rapids: Discovery House, 2010).

Books: Children and Families

Blackett Schlank, Christina, and Lonnie K. Zeltzer, *Conquering Your*

Child's Chronic Pain: A Pediatrician's Guide for Reclaiming a Normal Childhood (New York: Harper Paperbacks, 2005).

Bradford, Mary, and Elizabeth Hoekstra, *Chronic Kids, Constant Hope: Help and Encouragement for Parents of Children with Chronic Conditions* (Wheaton, IL: Crossway, 2005).

Cline, Foster W., and Lisa Greene, *Parenting Children with Health Issues: Essential Tools, Tips, and Tactics for Raising Kids with Chronic Illness, Medical Conditions, and Special Healthcare Needs* (Golden, CO: Love and Logic Press, 2007).

Dell Clark, Cindy, *In Sickness and in Play: Children Coping with Chronic Illness* (New Brunswick, NJ: Rutgers University Press, 2003).

Dell Orlo, Arthur E., and Paul W. Power, *Families Living with Chronic Illness and Disability* (New York: Springer, 2004).

———, *The Resilient Family: Living with Your Child's Illness or Disability* (Notre Dame, IN: Sorin, 2003).

Farrel, Bill, and Pam Farrel, *The Ten Best Decisions Every Family Can Make* (Eugene, OR: Harvest House, 2006).

Lowes, Lesley, and Fay Valentine, eds., *Nursing Care of Children and Young People with Chronic Illness* (Hoboken, NJ: Wiley-Blackwell, 2007).

Omartian, Stormie, *The Power of a Praying Parent Book of Prayers* (Eugene, OR: Harvest House, 2007).

Philo, Jolene, *A Different Dream for My Child: Meditations for Parents of Critically or Chronically Ill Children* (Grand Rapids: Discovery House, 2009).

———, *Different Dream Parenting: A Practical Guide to Raising a Child with Special Needs* (Grand Rapids: Discovery House, 2011).

Ward, Jonathan, and Lynda T. Young, *Hope for Families of Children with Cancer* (Abilene, TX: Leafwood, 2011).

Support for Children with Disabilities
Brave Kids
bravekids.org
An online resource center for children with disabilities or chronic, life-threatening illnesses that provides over 11,000 resources, medical information, and emotional support to children with special needs such as autism, cancer, cerebral palsy, ADD, and more.

Tufts University Child & Family Web Guide
www.cfw.tufts.edu
A directory that evaluates, describes and provides links to hundreds of sites containing child development research and practical advice.

Accreditation of Care Facilities
Accreditation Commission for Health Care
www.achc.org
919-785-1214

CareScout
Carescout.com
800-571-1918

National Association for Home Care and Hospice
www.nahc.org
202-547-7424

Nursing Home Compare Database, a service of Medicare
www.medicare.gov
800-633-4227

Housing and Home Resources
For local in-home support services, look in the blue government pages of the telephone directory under your county and Department of Human Services.

About: Senior Living
seniorliving.about.com

Affordable Apartment Search
www.hud.gov/apps/section8

Agenet: Solutions for better aging
www.age-net.co.uk

The American Association of Homes and Services for the Aging
http://healthfinder.gov/orgs/HR0456.htm

The Assisted Living Federation of America
www.alfa.org

The Consumer Consortium on Assisted Living
www.ccal.org
703-533-8121

Easy Connect/Early Bird Alert
www.earlybirdalert.com; 415-302-7691; info@earlybirdalert.com
A free healthcare hotline and app that helps seniors and the chronically ill connect to caregivers and designated healthcare providers by telephone, web, or mobile device.

Faith Hospice
faithhospicecare.org

The Hospice Foundation of America
www.hospicefoundation.org

Lotsa Helping Hands
Lotsahelpinghands.com
Free, private, web-based communities for organizing friends, family, and colleagues during times of need. Coordinate activities and manage volunteers with the group calendar.

National Adult Day Services Association
http://healthfinder.gov/orgs/HR3874.htm
887-745-1440

National Association for Home Care and Hospice
www.nahc.org
202-547-7424

Right at Home
www.rightathome.net

Senior Housing Locator
www.providerdata.com

Senior Resources Housing
www.seniorresource.com/house.htm

Associations, Organizations, and Services
AARP Driver Safety Course
www.AARP.org/families/driver_safety

Alzheimer's Association
www.alz.org
880-272-3900

Alzheimer's Daily News
www.agelessdesign.com

American Stroke Association
www.strokeassociation.org

The ARC: For people with intellectual and developmental
disabilities
www.thearc.org

Area Agency on Aging
www.n4a.org; look in the blue pages of your telephone directory
under "Guide to Human Services"

Department of Veterans Affairs
www.va.gov
800-829-1000

Gilda's Club
In a web search, type "Gilda's Club" and your city or state.

Hospice Link
www.hospiceworld.org
800-331-1620

Mayo Clinic Resources Online
www.mayoclinic.com

Meals on Wheels Association of America
www.mowaa.org
703-548-5558

Centers for Medicare and Medicaid Services
www.cms.gov

Meier Clinics
www.meierclinics.com
888-7CLINIC

Music for the Soul
www.musicforthesoul.org
National Academy of Elder Law Attorneys
www.naela.org
520-881-4005

National Alliance on Mental Illness
www.nami.org
800-950-NAMI

National Association of Professional Geriatric Care Managers
www.caremanager.org
520-881-8008

National Council on Aging
www.ncoa.org

National Hospice and Palliative Care Organization
www.nhpco.org
800-658-8898

National Multiple Sclerosis Society
www.nationalmssociety.org

PACE—Program of All-Inclusive Health for the Elderly
care-resources.org

Parkinson's Disease Foundation
www.pdf.org

Project Compassion
www.project-compassion.org

Rest Ministries
restministries.com

Social Security
www.ssa.gov

Stroke Family Support Network
888-478-7653

Veterans' Medical Services
877-222-VETS

Veterans of Foreign Wars Service Hotline
www.vfw.org
800-VFW-1899

Visiting Nurse Associations of America
www.vnaa.org
800-426-2547

The Volunteer Income Tax Assistance Program
800-829-1040

Caregiver Advocacy Groups
The Compassionate Friends
P.O. Box 3696
Oak Brook, IL 60522-3696
630-990-0010
www.compassionatefriends.org

Family Caregiver Alliance
690 Market Street, Suite 600
San Francisco, CA 94104
800-445-8106
415-434-3388
www.caregiver.org

Friends' Health Connection
P.O. Box 114
New Brunswick, NJ
800-48-FRIEND (483-7436)
732-418-1811
www.48friend.org

National Alliance for Caregiving
4720 Montgomery Lane, Suite 642
Bethesda, MD 20814-3425
301-718-8444
www.caregiving.org

National Caregiving Foundation
801 North Pitt Street, #116
Alexandria, VA 22314
800-930-1357
703-299-9300
www.caregivingfoundation.org

National Family Caregivers Association
10400 Connecticut Avenue, Suite 500
Kensington, MD 20895
800-896-3650
301-942-6430
www.nfcacares.org

Joni and Friends
International Disability Center
PO Box 3333
Agoura Hills, CA 91376-3333
www.joniandfriends.org

Rainbows
2100 Golf Road, #370
Rolling Meadows, IL 60008
800-266-3206
847-952-1770
www.rainbows.org

Rosalynn Carter Institute of Caregiving
Georgia Southwestern State University
800 Wheatley Street
Americus, GA 31709

912-928-1234
rci.gsw.edu

Well Spouse Association
63 West Main Street, Suite H
Freehold, NJ 07728
800-838-0879
732-577-8899
www.wellspouse.org

General Resources

American Academy of Family Physicians, "Stress: Helping Your Family Cope with Life's Challenges," *American Family Physician*, November 2000, http://www.aafp.org/afp/2000/1115/p2351 .html.

Beach, Shelly, *The Silent Seduction of Self-Talk: Conforming Deadly Thought Patterns to the Word of God* (Chicago: Moody Publishers, 2009).

Heim, Gary and Lisa, *True North: Choosing God in the Frustrations of Life* (Grand Rapids: Kregel, 2011).

Team Hoyt, www.teamhoyt.com.

Appendix 3

PRAYER GUIDES

Day One: *My Hope Is in God*

Wait for the Lord; be strong and take heart and wait for the Lord. (Psalm 27:14)

> *Gracious God, I can be confident in any circumstance because I find my strength in You. You are the Lord God, the King of heaven, and I choose to place my hope in You because You alone are worthy of my trust. I can take heart and come to You when my strength is gone. Even now, I wait for You, trusting You to work out what is best in Your time and Your way.*

Day Two: *Confession*

"For I will forgive their wickedness and will remember their sins no more." (Jeremiah 31:34)

> *Father God, You know I've sinned against You, and I confess my sins to You now. I've hurt others, myself, and You through my actions, and I am grieved over what I've done. Please forgive me, and give me wisdom and strength to make things right with those I've wronged. Heal those I've*

hurt. Thank You for Your mercy and grace given so freely through the shed blood of Your Son, Jesus.

Day Three: Attitudes

Above all else, guard your heart, for everything you do flows from it. (Proverbs 4:23 TNIV)

Lord, so often I'm blind to the anger and selfishness in my spirit. Help me to be willing to look deeply into my heart and to guard it. Let me root out every thought that sets itself against You and instead choose to apply a grid of truth to my thinking—to focus on what is true, honest, just, pure, lovely, of good report, and virtuous so that I can become more like Jesus.

Day Four: Desert Places

Though the fig tree does not bud and there are no grapes on the vines, though the olive crop fails and the fields produce no food, though there are no sheep in the pen and no cattle in the stalls, yet I will rejoice in the Lord, I will be joyful in God my Savior. (Habakkuk 3:17–18)

Dear God, sometimes it seems like my faith is dry and lifeless and all I hear in my prayers is silence. But faith tells me that You are there. I rejoice in Your presence and Your love for me. You can teach me even in the desert places if I choose to listen and learn. Today I choose joy in knowing Your love is constant and unchanging, forever fixed.

Day Five: Strength

I can do all this through him who gives me strength. (Philippians 4:13 TNIV)

Dear God, You are the provider of my strength. I come to You today asking for renewal of my body, soul, and spirit. Empower me through Your

Holy Spirit to do the things you have for me to do. My flesh and heart may fail, but my hope is in You. In this very moment, You are my shield, protecting me, and my sustenance. Renew my spirit and strengthen me for every good work, Father.

Day Six: Advice

But Rehoboam rejected the advice the elders gave him and consulted the young men who had grown up with him and were serving him. (1 Kings 12:8)

Dear Father, You are the source of all knowledge. I ask for Your Holy Spirit to move in me to discern good advice from bad among the counselors and advisors in my life so that I might bring You glory in the decisions I make. Give me wisdom to know what to do, and help me rest confidently in You.

Day Seven: Guilt

Show me your ways, O Lord, teach me your paths; guide me in your truth and teach me, for you are God my Savior, and my hope is in you all day long. (Psalm 25:4–5)

Dear Father, thank You for caring about my emotions. Help me to recognize false guilt and to reject it, along with unrealistic expectations others place upon me. Help me to rest in You for my acceptance. Give me a heart that is sensitive to Your leading and conviction that comes from Your Spirit.

Day Eight: Diagnosis and Dependency

Unless the Lord had given me help, I would soon have dwelt in the silence of death. When I said, "My foot is slipping," your love, O Lord, supported me. (Psalm 94:17–18)

Lord, I'm tempted to fear what I cannot see, know, or control. But my security rests in You and not in what happens to me or around me. Help me rest in Your unfailing love. You alone are my security and hope.

Day Nine: God Rules

"Remember the former things, those of long ago; I am God, and there is no other; I am God, and there is none like me. I make known the end from the beginning, from ancient times, what is still to come. I say, 'My purpose will stand, and I will do all that I please.'" (Isaiah 46:9–10)

Nothing can upset Your plan and purposes for my life, Father. I choose to trust in You and to thank You for Your faithfulness to all generations. Thank You for redeeming the things in my past, the things in my present, and the things that lie in my future.

Day Ten: Perseverance

For everything that was written in the past was written to teach us, so that through the endurance taught in the Scriptures and the encouragement they provide we might have hope. (Romans 15:4 TNIV)

Father, You bless those who delight in You. Even in my problems and trials, I will not be shaken because I trust in You and Your plan for my life. May I learn lessons of grace and obedience as I remain true to Your purposes and calling for me. Give me strength in times of testing. I bless Your name, Father.

Day Eleven: The Bigger Picture

. . . who through faith are shielded by God's power until the coming of the salvation that is ready to be revealed in the last time. In all this you greatly rejoice, though now for a little while you may have had to suffer grief in all kinds of trials. (1 Peter 1:5–6)

You've promised that suffering will be redeemed when Your eternal plan is revealed, Father. Thank You that I can trust that even my pain will be used to glorify You and to bring about Your plan in the world, in spite of what I may see in this moment.

Day Twelve: Worry

"Therefore do not worry about tomorrow, for tomorrow will worry about itself. Each day has enough trouble of its own." (Matthew 6:34)

Lord, I admit that I take things into my own hands and worry. Help me to trust You. I give You the glory as I lay down my burdens and turn to You. Lift the heaviness from my heart as I lean upon You.

Day Thirteen: Peace

Let the peace of Christ rule in your hearts, since as members of one body you were called to peace. And be thankful. (Colossians 3:15)

No matter my circumstances, I'm promised Your peace, Jesus, and I claim it as my own. Your peace is not dependent upon what I see, but is rooted in Your character and love. Thank You for providing peace that passes understanding for me today.

Day Fourteen: Anger

A person's wisdom yields patience; it is to one's glory to overlook an offense. (Proverbs 19:11 TNIV)

Father, sometimes I don't feel like overlooking incompetence or indifference or rudeness or pain. Sometimes I feel like indulging myself in a little attitude. May I employ discernment and be willing to lay down my rights to glorify You. May I be stirred by the things that stir Your heart.

Day Fifteen: Abiding

Your word is a lamp to my feet and a light for my path. (Psalm 119:105)

When I'm overwhelmed by change, transition, medical information, and counsel from well-intentioned friends and relatives, help me remember that Your Word offers the wisdom I need on the path You've set before me. In moments when I'm fearful about decisions and circumstances, help me remember that Your Word and Your Spirit sustain me.

Day Sixteen: Pain

Surely he took up our pain and bore our suffering, yet we considered him punished by God, stricken by him, and afflicted. (Isaiah 53:4 TNIV)

Dear Father, Your Son Jesus willingly bore our sins and carried our sorrows. He was moved with such deep sorrow that He wept over our pain and died to bear it. Thank You that we have a great high priest who has conquered—Jesus, the Son of God. I have hope for today because Jesus loves me so much and I can trust Him, even in my deepest pain.

Day Seventeen: Answered Prayer

I sought the Lord, and he answered me; he delivered me from all my fears. (Psalm 34:4)

Father God, I have prayed, and You have answered me; You delivered me from all my fears. You answered me in the day of my distress and have been with me wherever I have gone. I love You, Lord, for You hear my voice and my cry for mercy. You turn Your ear to me. I will call on You as long as I live. Lord, You are my strength and shield; my heart trusts in You, and I am helped.

Day Eighteen: Death

Precious in the sight of the Lord is the death of his saints. (Psalm 116:15)

Father God, You tell us that the death of Your saints is precious to You. You promise to be our God forever and to be our guide to the end. Even though I walk through the valley of the shadow of death, I will fear no evil, because You are with me. You are always with me; You hold me by my right hand. You guide me with Your counsel, and afterward You promise to take me into glory. Who do I have in heaven but You? I desire nothing on earth besides You. My body and my heart may fail, but You are the strength of my heart and my portion forever.

Day Nineteen: The Lord Is with You

The Lord, the King of Israel, is with you; never again will you fear any harm. (Zephaniah 3:15)

Dear Father, You are the Lord of heaven, the King of Israel, and You have promised to be with me. I don't have to fear or be dismayed, for You are my God. You strengthen me and help me. You uphold me with Your righteous right hand. You strengthen weak hands and weak knees that give way. You say to the fearful, "Be strong, do not fear," because You promise to come to save us. You are with me, and You are mighty to save. You take great delight in me and quiet me with Your love. You rejoice over me with singing, Lord, like a father singing a lullaby over his child. Thank You for Your tender love for me.

Day Twenty: Fear

The Lord is my light and my salvation—whom shall I fear? The Lord is the stronghold of my life—of whom shall I be afraid? (Psalm 27:1)

God, in every situation, You are my protection and salvation. I have nothing to fear. You are my stronghold and defender. Fear has no hold on me because my strength is in You.

Day Twenty-one: Coming Back

Once again David inquired of the Lord, and the Lord answered him. (1 Samuel 23:4)

Lord, sometimes my heart wanders away. Please draw me back to You, no matter where I've been or what I've done. Don't let arrogance or indifference take root in my heart. May my heart forever be dependent upon You. Create a clean heart in me, O God, and renew a right spirit within me.

Day Twenty-two: Anxiety

Anxiety weighs down the heart, but a kind word cheers it up. (Proverbs 12:25 TNIV)

Dear Father, Your Word tells us that anxiety weighs us down. It fills our days with pain and grief and robs our nights of rest. It's worthless. Jesus assures me that my heart doesn't have to be troubled when my trust is placed in You, Jehovah God, and in Your Son. I don't have to be anxious about anything. I can present my prayers and petitions to You directly. Father, today I ask for Your peace that transcends all understanding. Let it guard my heart and my mind through the power of your Son, Jesus.

Day Twenty-three: Courage

I remain confident of this: I will see the goodness of the Lord in the land of the living. Wait for the Lord; be strong and take heart and wait for the Lord. (Psalm 27:13–14 TNIV)

Dear Father, I admit that there are days when I do not feel courageous or brave. But I place my confidence in You, in Your goodness, and in Your character as the good and righteous and loving God of mercy.

Day Twenty-four: Depression

Then I called on the name of the Lord: "O Lord, save me!" (Psalm 116:4)

Dear Father, I feel vulnerable and weak, but You are my refuge and strength, my help in trouble. I call upon Your name, Lord. Save me from despair. Help me overcome sadness and depression so that I may bring glory to Your name and proclaim Your favor.

Day Twenty-five: Healing

Heal me, O Lord, and I will be healed; save me and I will be saved, for you are the one I praise. (Jeremiah 17:14)

Father God, You are the Great Physician, and I ask for healing, whether in mind, body, spirit, or in all of these. I ask, believing, and I trust You to give what is best. Thank You for Your goodness, kindness, and love in all things and for the blessings You have brought into my life.

Day Twenty-six: Prayer

Pray continually; give thanks in all circumstances, for this is God's will for you in Christ Jesus. (1 Thessalonians 5:17–18)

Even when I do not feel thankful, dear Father, I choose thanks. You are with me every moment and in every circumstance; Your presence surrounds me. Thank You for caring about every detail of my life.

Day Twenty-seven: Brokenness

They all ate and were satisfied, and the disciples picked up twelve basketfuls of broken pieces of bread and fish. (Mark 6:42–43)

> *Dear Father, You promise purpose in our pain. Take the broken pieces of my life and multiply them the way You multiplied the loaves and fish. Don't let them go to waste, but use them to feed others, heal them, and show them Your glory and Your amazing love.*

Day Twenty-eight: Numbering Our Days

Teach us to number our days, that we may gain a heart of wisdom. (Psalm 90:12 TNIV)

> *Lord, teach me to number my days and to live each day to the fullest. Show me what You desire of me today, and give me wisdom and joy in fulfilling those things.*

Day Twenty-nine: Mourning

Those who sow with tears will reap with songs of joy. Those who go out weeping, carrying seed to sow, will return with songs of joy, carrying sheaves with them. (Psalm 126:5–6 TNIV)

> *Jesus, You said that those who mourn are blessed and will be comforted. In my sorrow, I'm reaching out to You for comfort and strength. Give me grace to respond to my suffering with a patient and loving attitude so that I bring honor to Your name.*

Day Thirty: Blessing

"Whoever believes in me, as Scripture has said, rivers of living water will flow from within them." (John 7:38 TNIV)

Dear Father, make me a conduit of living water to those around me. May streams of blessing, life, truth, and grace flow from me so that others may see Jesus when they look at me. Clean out the silt and sludge that keeps the water from flowing. May I channel Your character and love, and direct people to You in all I do and say.

Prayers for a Transformed Spirit

Pray through the topics below. Ask God to increase your sensitivity to the leading of the Holy Spirit and to renew a God-honoring spirit in your heart as you seek a fresh beginning with each new day. Pray, "Dear Father, by the power of Your Holy Spirit, renew in me . . ."

a whole-hearted spirit	*Numbers 14:24*
a spirit of wisdom	*Deuteronomy 34:9*
a teachable spirit	*Psalm 25:4–5*
joy in the Lord	*Psalm 33:1*
delight in the Lord	*Psalm 37:4*
rest in the Lord	*Psalm 37:7*
steadfast spirit	*Psalm 51:10*
a willing spirit	*Psalm 51:12*
a humble and contrite spirit	*Psalm 51:17*
an undivided heart and new spirit	*Psalm 86:11; Ezekiel 36:26*
longing for God	*Isaiah 26:9*
a spirit of praise	*Isaiah 61:3*
a servant's heart	*Mark 10:44–45*
a worshiping spirit	*John 4:24*
a spirit of repentance	*Acts 26:20*
strength in spirit	*Ephesians 3:16*
a spirit of edification	*Ephesians 4:29*
a spirit of forgiveness	*Ephesians 4:32*
renewal/filling of the Holy Spirit	*Ephesians 5:18*

a grateful spirit	*Ephesians 5:20*
a spirit of unity with the church	*Philippians 2:1–8; Romans 15:5–7*
a yielded spirit	*Philippians 2:5–8*
a spirit of love	*2 Timothy 1:7; 1 Corinthians 13:3–8*
a spirit of self-control	*2 Timothy 1:7*
faith	*Hebrews 11:6*
a quiet and gentle spirit	*1 Peter 3:4*
a spirit of truth	*1 John 4:6*
a return to my first love	*Revelation 2:4–5; 3:18–20*

Letters from the Heart of God

These letters show how the Word of God can be personally applied to our hearts as love letters from God.[1] As you read them, consider how you might write your own, applying specific Scripture passages. Then pour out your heart in a prayer of love and worship to God.

My Precious One,

Come to me. I am waiting for you in this very moment with open arms. I long to embrace you with My unfailing love. Even now I am sustaining you, strengthening you in body, soul, and spirit for this season of your life.

Know that this season of pain is temporary, and I am beside you in every moment. I will never abandon you. My grace is sufficient for your need. My precious one, no matter who may or may not stand at your side from day to day loving and caring for you, I am your all-sustaining caregiver.

I know your deepest fears in the darkness of night—those things that rob you of rest. I know your fears of change, of dependency, of an unknown future and a certain future; I

---

1. Based on Annetta Dellinger and Karen Boerger, *JOY-spirations for Caregivers* (Winepress, 2010).

know your regret for things unspoken and things spoken, for dreams that might never be fulfilled. I know the thoughts that course through you on discouraging days and the frustrations you've swept into a dark corner of your heart.

Come to me, my precious one. My arms are open, and I long to listen to your burdened heart.

Your Loving Father

My Precious One,

Your heart is nearly bursting—I can see it. I want you to know you can run into my throne room with boldness and cry out for the grace, strength, and power you need. Don't sit outside the door—run into My presence like a child who simply *must* see her father.

In My presence is fullness of joy. As you sit with Me, your true caregiver, you'll find sustaining hope for your circumstances. My Word is My love letter to you, and in its pages I share My heart: I'm faithful. I'll meet your needs. I'll never leave you or forsake you. I'll give you joy, even when things look hopeless and you don't understand.

You may never understand the reasons why things happen in your life. Even Jesus asked me *Why?*—not because He questioned my authority but because He was expressing the deep pain and suffering He felt on behalf of a sinful world.

You carry heavy burdens, my child. Bring them to me. I am waiting. I am and have all you will ever need.

Your Loving Father

Appendix 4

When to Call Hospice

At one time, the term "hospice" referred to a place where weary travelers could take shelter. Today, hospice refers to a unique type of care provided to patients nearing the end of life.

Hospice services concentrate on pain relief and symptom management for persons who are no longer receiving curative treatment. Hospice addresses the needs of the whole person—physical, emotional, and spiritual—as well as providing support to family members, loved ones, and caregivers.

The best time to call hospice is soon after receiving a life-limiting diagnosis. The earlier hospice care is initiated, the sooner pain and symptoms can be brought under control. When started early, hospice care can ensure the patient's mental, emotional, and physical comfort and quality of life, and provide support to family and caregivers.

The following are signs that it's time to discuss hospice care with the patient's physician or caregivers.

- A gradual decline in the patient's level of functioning is observed.
- The patient requires increasing visits to the emergency room, hospital, or doctor's office.

- The disease is progressing or spreading.
- The condition is life-limiting and a cure is not possible.
- The patient's level of functioning declines in spite of therapy.
- The patient loses interest in eating or may have stopped eating completely.
- Unintentional weight loss continues.
- The patient has end-stage dementia and is no longer mobile.
- The patient voices a desire for comfort care.
- Family or caregivers desire help with end-of-life issues.
- Care is becoming more difficult to manage.[1]

1. Used by permission of Faith Hospice, 2100 Raybrook SE, Suite 300, Grand Rapids, MI 49546, 616-235-5100.

Appendix 5

When Forgiveness Is Hard

The issue of forgiveness is complex. On the one hand, we forgive for the benefits we receive, and on the other hand, we forgive because forgiveness confronts sin as Jesus confronted sin and offers grace as an alternative response.

Here are some benefits of forgiving others.

+ **Forgiveness gives us physical and emotional benefits.** Research studies show that dopamine, the biochemical that raises our sense of pleasure, and serotonin, which elevates our mood, both rise when we forgive others.
+ **Forgiveness frees us.** Forgiveness allows us to rid ourselves of anger, and in that sense, frees us from being under the power of someone else. It breaks the chains that hold us to our past.
+ **Forgiveness allows us to conquer evil.** The weapon we're given to conquer evil is the power of doing good. God's Word promises us in Genesis 3:15 that in the end, evil will be crushed under Jesus' feet in God's final retribution. Until then, our weapon against evil is our power to do good against even our enemies. Forgiveness is a radical act of defiance against evil.

♦ **Forgiveness releases us from the power of others.** Acts of retaliation tell our abusers they still have power over us—the power to control us and to perpetuate the cycle of hate within us. Forgiveness gives us the power to act freely and to break the power of our abusers. Forgiveness tells our abusers, "I'm not running from you. Your sin won't work here. In forgiving you, I'm dismantling your works of evil."[1]

---

1. Based on an interview with Dr. Dan Allender, Rod VanSolkema, and Tim Jackson, *Help for My Life*, 2009, available at http://www.helpformylife.org/Forgiveness%20-%20Overcoming%20Evil%20With%20Good.aspx.

Appendix 6

STEPS TO BANISHING BITTERNESS

Identify the target of your bitterness. We often become bitter at God when we believe He's given us a raw deal or He's unjust. We become angry. We typically become bitter at other people when we believe they've wronged us or betrayed us. And we can become bitter at ourselves when we believe we've failed or messed up.

Understand that people usually don't see their bitterness. Hebrews 12:15 tells us, "See to it that no one misses the grace of God and that no bitter root grows up to cause trouble and defile many." We're usually blind to our own problem with bitterness.

Acknowledge and confess your bitter spirit. Ask God to forgive you of the sin of bitterness and resentment. Then ask Him to help you forgive those you've harbored anger against. Matthew 6:14 tells us that if we don't forgive others, God will use the same measuring stick with us.

Work on bitterness you may hold toward God. Trust His wisdom. We live in a sinful world, but God promises that justice will win, and He will work things for good (Romans 8:28). Ask God what He wants to teach you through your circumstances. Apply the principles of God's Word to your situation. Reject a victim mentality and develop an attitude of gratitude. Inventory what you've been given and learn the power of praise.

Work on bitterness you may hold toward others. Keep short accounts with others—Scripture tells us to set things straight before the sun goes down (Ephesians 4:26). Keep a guard on your tongue, and don't take pleasure in the downfall of others. Let God be responsible for justice. We're instructed to pursue peace (1 Peter 3:11).

Finally, let it go. When you forgive, let an offense become part of history and refuse to bring it up again. Pray for those who've hurt you. Ask God to give you Jesus' eyes and heart toward that individual. The power of prayer can change your heart.

Work on bitterness you may hold toward yourself. Who does God say you are? Do you believe it? Refuse to focus on the past. Be sure you've confessed past sin and set things straight with those you may have wronged, and then forgive yourself. Your sins are gone.

Acknowledgments

It's impossible for me to thank all the people who have influenced me and contributed to the creation of this book. Special and heartfelt thanks to Carol Holquist, Judith Markham, and Miranda Gardner, the publishing and editorial staff at Discovery House Publishers who have honed me into a better writer and given me the opportunity to share my message with people across the globe. You all share a special place in my heart.

Thank you to Tim Beals, my agent, who brought this project to Discovery House and shares my vision and passion for the caregiving community.

Thank you to the Guild—Ann Byle, Sharron Carrns, Cynthia Beach, Angela Blycker, Allison Hodgson, Lorilee Craker, and Tracy Groot. You are my warrior-sisters of the word, and I am forever grateful for you.

Thank you Blythefield Hills Church for the energizing teaching of the Word that equips me to write, teach, and speak. Your leadership, teaching, and equipping empowers all that I do.

Special thanks to my family, who supports me and loves me and is forever patient, whether I'm staring wordlessly at a screen, traveling, or distracted by thoughts about the next chapter or book. Mountains of thanks to Dan, the most loving and supportive husband in the world; to daughter Jessica and dear son-in-law Mosiah; to son Nate and sweet daughter-in-law Allison; and to Wanda, dear sister-friend.

NOTE TO THE READER

The publisher invites you to share your response to the message of this book by writing Discovery House Publishers, P.O. Box 3566, Grand Rapids, MI 49501, U.S.A. For information about other Discovery House books, music, videos, or DVDs, contact us at the same address or call 1-800-653-8333. Find us on the Internet at www.dhp.org or send e-mail to books@dhp.org.